Achieving True Democracy

A New Breed of Party as Realistic Next Step

Peter Monien

IMPRINT

DEDICATION

For all who think that handing out blank political cheques for four years can't be our best idea how democracy can work.

#UpgradingDemocracy

#FixDemocracyFirst

#EndPoliticalApathy

#PoliticalRepresentation

#DirectDemocracy

#Decentralization

#GameB

This version 1.0 of my book represents my current thoughts on the topic. I hope that it can be used as a starting point to kindle more discussions from other like-minded individuals. What is important, though, is the guiding principle presented behind the words in this book, not the words themselves.

CONTENT

INTRODUCTION:
POLITICS DOESN'T REPRESENT US

Politics doesn't represent the majority of the People. Public opinion and public policy differ, sometimes a lot. Even if an overwhelming majority is clearly in favor of a certain policy it doesn't mean that this will translate to legislative action in parliament.

A 'good' example are the two US-parties locked in a partisan death spiral. Without them the US population could easily agree on dozens of issues listed in the article *What if a Presidential Candidate Ran on What Most Americans Actually Wanted?*[1]

An American study has shown that "when preferences of low- or middle-income Americans diverge from those of the affluent, there is virtually no relationship between policy outcomes and the desires of less advantaged groups."[2] A German study revealed very similar results.[3]

Worldwide, the currently implemented democratic systems and their rules seem to work against a democratic representation. The systems themselves and their rules were formed by professional politicians over decades, and the only people who can change this situation are those politicians themselves.

A catch-22 situation

Whenever we try to break this cycle and go the direct way and get a new party elected into parliament, we recognize that this is very hard. The political rules are set up against new political parties. Yet when we succeed, this new party seems to warp into the same stuff that our established parties are made from.

Whenever we try this indirectly and put pressure on them via NGOs and other groups, we recognize that this is very hard. Of the issues that are neglected by our politicians, there are only a few that we can take forward. For every hard-earned victory, there seem to be 10 additional things that someone should fight for. We simply lag the time and resources to keep up with all of the new laws and regulations we are bombarded with or the topics neglected by our politicians.

Slowly but surely, democracy itself is losing ground
Actually, in times of COVID-19, we lose ground fast. The speed of dismantling basic rights that we thought sacrosanct is breathtaking. Authoritarian regulations have grown fast in the shadow of 9-11 and now make a great leap forward and put civil rights and democracy itself at risk. The 'pandemic shock doctrine' works well and seems to keep most of the world's citizens in a Stockholm syndrome light.

While dismantling our basic rights many current political parties act undemocratically or even anti-democratically by weakening the separation of powers, suppressing transparency, obfuscating accountability, decreasing control, etc.

Democracy itself and its institutions are at risk
Because of the work of these political parties over decades, trust in politics, in democratic institutions, and in democracy itself is at an all-time low. The *Global Satisfaction with Democracy Report 2020* shows a 57.5% share of dissatisfied people in 2020.[4] And it is this trust on which our civilization is ultimately built.

It is time to upgrade democracy
Yes, it is true: most political systems worldwide are rigged and not constructed to represent the majority.

But the solution is not to replace democracy with a strong man and destroy democratic institutions. Instead, we have to find a lever and fix and improve our democratic system and institutions.

This short book focusses on the parliamentarian realm. It outlines a solution to actively create what we need: a people's champion in parliament who truly speaks for them and cannot be bought by big money.

To be able to achieve this, we must rethink the very concept of the political party as a vehicle for representing democratic interests.

This breed type of grassroots democratic party will effectively and efficiently...

> ...focus on bringing real democracy and transparency,
>
> ...ensure and proof that its internal democratic processes are kept,
>
> ...use well-balanced facts instead of manipulative inputs,
>
> ...focus on common ground to advance the public good,
>
> ...give its members the decision and
>
> ...focus on the 1:1 representation of its members.

This new type of party not only (largely) solves the problem of our representation crisis, but also offers solutions to other problems of representative democracy:

- Participatory determination of party issues and their prioritization, instead of predefined, inflexible packages of issues and solutions offered by traditional parties
- Integration of a process to identify and address neglected issues
- Better traceability of internal decision-making processes
- Faster democratic voting on more issues

All of this sounds too lofty and too good to be true?

I can assure you, that this new breed of party is not only thinkable but also implementable in the current political system.

PART I

THE PROXY PARTY

A NEW BREED OF POLITICAL PARTY
THE PROXY PARTY

As long as we don't fix the political system itself, the system will not represent us. Therefore, democracy itself needs an upgrade. Urgently!

If we are serious about strengthening democracy within the next years and achieve true representation, we must rethink the political party as a vehicle for representing democratic interests. The new breed of political party shouldn't impose its political will on its members but only assist them to form their individual political will and represent this as accurately as possible. It will not force a decision by majority vote but truly represent the breadth of decisions its members reached after consideration of the topic.

Why do I call this new type of party "Proxy Party?"
Those familiar with information technology are certainly familiar with the word 'proxy' (server), that passes on information without changing it. In other words: it offers the best representation of the originator's message.

Assisting its members to form their individual political will
Some argue that direct democracy is a bad idea as simply leaving the decision to ill-informed party members wouldn't lead to better results. Actually, they have a point that this would put us at risk of rash decisions and oppression by the majority and partisan media as conductor of (often) constructed pictures and emotions.

To have a truly better solution we need to add fact-checking and deliberation. Only well balanced and structured input combined with a deliberative process enables a sound basis for thoughtful decisions that don't simply tap into our political reflexes and can lead to better results.

Thus, the Proxy Party also needs to facilitate the process of forming the individual political will. It can:

> …draw on the wisdom of crowds and specialists to structure the topic and bring in the relevant facts (with a clear distinction between facts and opinions),
> …check the facts and their originations,
> …create a short well-balanced overview paper of the topic (with references) as a decision basis,
> …create a culture to separate facts from their interpretation (facts first, discussion later) and
> …create a culture of thoughtful deliberation with a focus on mutual respect, common ground and interests instead of a rhetoric of demonization

Deliver proof that the party can be trusted

As trust in political parties has been mostly squandered in the last decades, it is not enough to promise to be different. The new party has to be able to prove that it is different and act very transparently to be able to convince voters. The party should go beyond the normal and should be able to prove (internally and externally) that it adhered to processes of fact gathering, discussion and representation. It should be able to exceed expectations and provide evidence of maintaining the integrity of the processes and of the results.

Information processes to ensure a sound decision basis:

- correctness of the provided basis data incl. source checking
- completeness of the most important facts and arguments (90:10 approach as you will not be able to achieve 100%)
- well-balanced input and comparison of arguments

Publish results of information processes and democratic processes:

> Audited content input
> + Checked compliance of adherence to the processes
> + Non-modifiable publication of test of contents and results
> = Verifiable safeguarding of decision documents

Grassroot democratic yet efficient

Some argue that a grassroot democratic organization will be fully occupied wasting time internally and will never be able to act effectively as a representative of its members. Looking at historic examples, they are mostly right.

Being a grassroot democratic organization and being effective or even efficient is an oxymoron. When everybody wants to discuss everything with everybody, discussions will not end. Even if a consensus is reached, new members will want to reopen topics and discuss them again.

The simple solution: only the party's program and the candidates need to be discussed and agreed on by all of its members. Afterward, the party should act as a normal party with 'direct democracy as exception.'

I argue that the members should let their appointed representatives work and should only interfere:

> …when the representatives' decisions can't be deducted from the program
> or
> …when they think that the proposed decisions of their representatives don't represent the spirit of the party program.

I further argue that this 'direct democracy by exception' needs a qualifier and propose a 5% hurdle of votes of all members that must be achieved to take the voting in the hands of the members. Of cause, this presupposes that members are timely informed about the decisions of their representatives before the vote in parliament. Technology will then be required to safely and efficiently collect the votes.

I argue that the party's program should be split into two parts:

- The core program should be concerned with the core topics of the party: democracy and transparency. It should also contain the other fundamental values of the party.
- The extended part of the program should be concerned with everything else the members agree on.

I will discuss the reasons for this proposal, and why it increases the effectiveness and efficiency of the proxy party, later in the book.

Furthermore, the Proxy Party must be very focused on its culture and processes.

Culture:

- focused on facts and results
- providing high-quality well-balanced overview decision papers
- civilized respectful deliberation but no restricting 'political correctness'
- aiming to reach consensus on common interests

Processes:

- grassroot democratic creation and amendment of the party's program
- strict adherence to processes of gathering data, checking data, deliberation, and decision
- most accurate representation of its members voting ratio in parliament

Overview: The three pillars of the Proxy Party

As described and further detailed in the coming chapters of this short book, the party officials would be able to act as efficient as 'normal' party officials. The only difference would be that they have to provide their decisions upfront to their members. This is where the 'direct democracy by exception' comes in.

Procedures can indeed become somewhat more complex than in a conventional party, as elected representatives have the additional burden of informing their members in advance of their vote. But I would also argue that they will be far more effective to represent their members as they constantly touch base and seek input from them.

You could describe the main democratic process of the Proxy Party in the following three steps:

1. The members are able to take voting in their own hands with a 5% takeover vote to transfer the topic to the party internal structured deliberation process.

2. The topic specialists and facilitators will provide a sound basis for well-informed deliberation and decision. The topic specialists will gather and check facts and provide a well-balanced input paper. The facilitators will oversee a civilized added-value focused respectful deliberation process.

3. The best possible representation of the members base by a 1:1 transfer to parliament: the elected representatives will vote according to the voting

ratio of the members. If 80% of the members vote for YES and 20% for NO, eight of 10 representatives will vote for YES and two of 10 representatives will vote for NO, no representative will abstain.

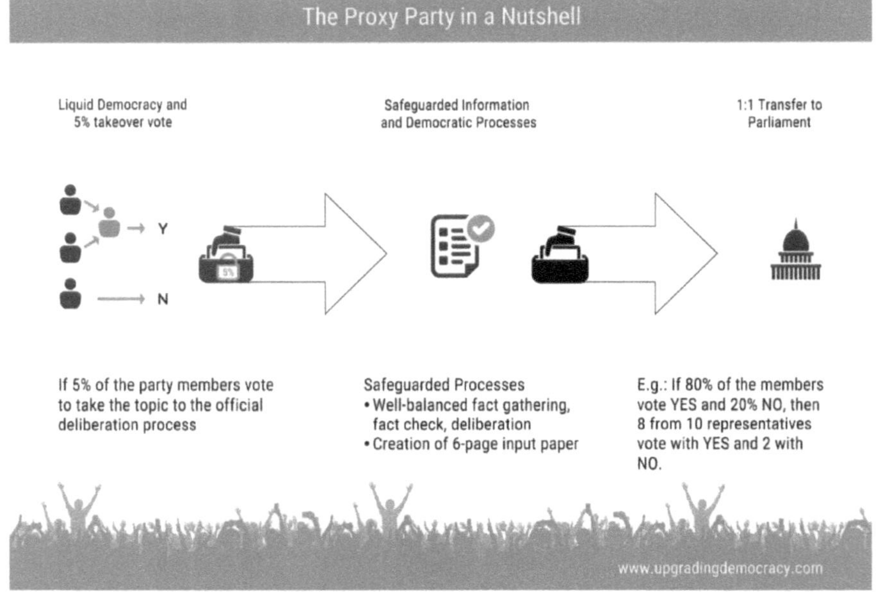

The People's Participation Party

The role for the party member will change from handing out blank checks for complete policy package deals to having a real say in each decision and truly is the sovereign. The new system offers a change from a one-time act of democracy every few years to a constant option to take back control.

Citizens who want to get politically involved can do so in a targeted manner in the new Proxy Party. This is not a matter of joining the 'conventional political tour' and through party obedience, but rather of one's own competence in the subject matter and convincing argumentation. In the proxy party it is not the rank of a person that counts, but the power of the argument.

Citizens who don't want to actively involve themselves but would like to have a say in the decision-making process can do this far better than in any other party. Together with others, they can vote to take a decision at the member level. They can trust the preparatory information to be accurate and well-balanced as it is based on secured processes.

A SOUND BASIS AND
NEW PARTY OPERATING SYSTEM

The Proxy Party could give itself the normal type of program like a normal political party. But I would argue that it should go a different route to emphasize that. This route includes:

> ...the Proxy Party is more trustworthy,
>
> ...will be more open and adaptable to add topics based on the will and current priorities and their members and
>
> ...will ensure it will stay to be more representative than the conventional parties.

Why a party program at all?
A program should achieve the goal to rally people around a set of values and goals and enable its officials and elected representatives in parliament to act efficiently guided by this program.

A new party could decide not to have a party program at all. It could 'simply' ask its members or even all politically interested persons to give input and could aggregate this and drive forward these topics according to demand.

This would send a message to all politically interested that there is a new party in town that truly listens and will take care of these topics. But there were many new parties that promised to listen and act in the last years and decades.

I argue that this approach without an explicit program would only go half the way as the mass input will only be converted into good politics if the democratic process in the new party is not distorted like in the conventional parties.

It will only have a chance to achieve a meaningful democratic change if it puts safeguards in place for the information and democratic processes. It will be only trustworthy if it acts far more transparently than the conventional parties.

My argument is that the implicit rules that everybody agrees on should be made explicit.

After all, we all long for a new party that listens to us, doesn't take silence as consent, doesn't select facts like it pleases it (or even make them up), doesn't lie to us, follows democratic rules internally and is transparent so that we can check all of these preconditions for a good political process. Let's agree on these values as ground rules! Otherwise, the new party would miss out on the chance to signal that it will be a fully better and trustworthy democratic alternative. A promise to be different and to listen is not enough. We need guarantees for democracy and transparency outlined as a very specific party program to finally have a trustworthy partner in parliament.

I propose to split the party program into two separate parts: the core program and the extended program.

This thematic restriction underlines the focus to provide a new breed of political party as a better democratic alternative. It offers a commitment to fundamental social values and is at the same time open to current issues and decisions. It focusses on the core promise of the Proxy Party: a good representation based on well-balanced facts and a truly democratic process. It also prevents the party from deterring potential members or voters in the initial phase by prematurely selecting topics and future proofs of the party.

The reason for the split of the program
The main reason for the proposed split of the program is the establishment of common ground. We are all in desperate need of real representation. Instead of hoping for the best and see democracy dwindle, we have to take care of this ourselves.

We can install new ground rules that form the rules for future political representation and offer a better alternative to the existing party system that forces us to hand out blank checks to members of a profession that have proven untrustworthy many times in the past. We should offer a better alternative:

> "You never change things by fighting the existing reality. To change something, build a better new model that makes the existing model obsolete."
> -Buckminster Fuller

The core program should be constructed as a kind of new 'ground rules' or 'operating system' for political parties. It should focus on democracy, transparency, fact-checking, deliberative and democratic processes and true representation.

Of cause, you could just write internal rules and duplicate the text and incorporate this into a normal party program. But this wouldn't achieve the same as ..

> .. this 'normal procedure' would not underline the importance of this democratic upgrade as a prerequisite to be able to achieve all other goals and
> .. would mix the core values with the other topics and would thus abandon the chance to split the party program in a more fixed part (e.g. approval of 75%) and a more flexible part (e.g. 60%).

In the best case, these new ground rules will act as a seal of trustworthiness for parties that chose to play the higher democratic game with the true meaningful participation of its members.

In theory, all of the alternative political parties could unite under the roof of a new Proxy Party, agree on these ground rules, and build a better alternative for representation. All groups could agree on transparency, focusing on facts and deliberation based on these facts, informed decisions, true co-determination (with the 5% takeover vote), and representation with a 1:1 transfer of votes to parliament and form one strong alternative to the conventional parties.

How should the core program be determined?

The core program is the operating system for the new party. It needs to be decided by a broad majority of the members, e.g. 80% of present votes with a minimum of 60% of total existing votes. By deciding on the core program, the members give themselves and their representatives rules to follow.

I would suggest that later changes to it can be only made by a two-thirds majority vote or even 75% or even 80% and with at least 50% of total existing votes. The challenge, especially at the very beginning, will be to formulate these rules specific enough but also flexible enough as they certainly will have to be adapted according to experiences made to optimize for efficiency and effectiveness.

What should go inside the core program?
All of the mentioned points below are only a first approximation of the texts that should go inside the core program. These should aim to establish the ground rules for a trustworthy political party, that facilitates fact-based, well-balanced, deliberative processes to help its members to form their individual, well-informed political mind independently and its 1:1 representation in parliament.

> **Purpose of the Party and Grassroot Democracy:** The Proxy Party aims to improve democracy and the direct representation of voters. From the point of view of the situation at the time of the founding of the party, it considers the next step to be the supplementation of representative democracy with a meaningful direct-democratic corrective.
>
> The party will assist its members to form their individual political will based on checked well-balanced facts and deliberative processes and will represent their will 1:1 in parliament. It will strive to add strong direct-democratic elements to the representative political system, strengthen the system's resistance to undemocratic influences and remove existing rules and such that hinder a fair democratic representation of voters. The party will work to achieve true democratic separation of powers, namely the three pillars of democracy: executive, legislative, and judiciary, and its fourth unofficial pillar: media.
>
> The party is a grassroot democracy. The party officials act as representatives of its members. The members have the right to insist that decisions have to be taken by the basis of a qualified takeover vote. This starts a pre-defined process gathering of well-balanced facts, fact-checking and deliberation. All elected representatives of the party are bound to represent the results of this process as accurately as possible in parliament.
>
> The party will strive to install referendums and popular initiatives at all state levels with uniform, reasonable hurdles, full transparency, fact-checked input papers and multiple mandatory planning cells of 25 randomly drawn representative citizens independently evaluating the proposal. The results of the discussion of the cells and their recommendations will become part of the official voting documents sent to the voters.

The party will work to implement ranked-choice voting to make tactical voting unnecessary and achieve a far better translation of the will of the voters to elected parties/representatives.

Transparency – The party is transparent internally and externally as "sunlight is the best disinfectant" and transparency is the best preventive measure against patronage, corruption, and other abuses. It will install systems that prove its' adherence to its rules for well-balanced fact gathering, fact-checking, information preparation, deliberation, voting and representation.

The party and especially its officials and spoke persons will strive to use clear language that reflects the issues as they are instead of giving them a distorted meaning. Some ideas for the core topics democracy/transparency to think about for concrete ideas that a Proxy Party might be able to agree on include:

New Rules for Politicians: Make income statements of all elected representatives public, grade of accuracy: $10,000. Prohibition of the acceptance of lecture fees during the active term of office. A three-year ban on any lobbying activities for high-ranking parliamentarians who leave office. Establishment of an approval commission.

Lobbyists: create a mandatory lobby register with strict rules (whom it applies to, required data and transparency to provide, sanctions for misconduct, etc.). Lobbyists can talk with politicians, but they can't give them money. Paid lobbyists can't work in ministries. Have an introduction of a publicly accessible register of meetings with lobbyists for every elected representative (attendees, topics, time).

Party Financing: ban on corporate donations. No hidden financing through advertising in party newspapers or stands at party conferences or the like. Restriction of private donations to $500 per person per year. Better: Conversion of party financing to a system financed exclusively by the voters, whereby each citizen receives five $20 vouchers for each election. Unused vouchers go in a fund for election system improvement projects. Create a mandatory real-time register for party donations.

Decisions on their own behalf: establish laws for the financing of the parties and/or the delegates (deciding on their own behalf) come into power only in the next legislative period. This vote has to be pre-approved by the member base of the Proxy Party.

Control the State: install an independent central unit for whistle-blowers on the federal and state level that acts against the misuse of state power. A blockchain-based log for access to personal data by authorities. There will be only logged access with registered proof of a judge authorizing it. Shorter archiving periods to allow for a timelier political reappraisal.

New Rules for Parliament:

- Establish a documented 'legislative footprint' who gave input or otherwise influenced the creation of a draft bill or regulation, etc.
- Ban lobbyists from pre-writing laws and implementation of strict rules for exclusion of representatives from votes that have conflicts of interest as described in my book Upgrading Democracy.
- Well-balanced allocation of speaking rights and time by the members and not by the chairmen of political groups and banning of the obligation to follow your political group (whip) but opening towards grassroot democratic votes.
- Tightening of laws so that a minimum number of representatives must be present during votes.
- Banning of ad-hoc votes to allow for due preparation.

On the last two points mentioned above, a very narrow definition of exceptions should be given in order not to undermine the democratic control weights; the explicit consent of the Chairman of the Assembly is required.

New Rules for Drafting Laws and Laws: Transfer of the preparation of legislative papers to an independent policy assessment department that acts as 'impartial judge' and prepares each case for/against changes of laws incl. an internal group that is vetting factuality, reason and balance. "This would ensure that the debates improve in quality, accuracy and accountability. That is, for each new law, independently create a publicly available case for and against, based on vetted contributions from all interested, including any costs and risks of change. Then have all of our legislators take the time in parliament to hear the vetted evidence and reasoning within those cases and make an informed and well-considered collective decision."[5]

Automatic sunset clauses for all changes. The results of the change have to be measured against the expected effects. The measurement has to adhere to a predefined framework. If ever possible, a change has to be trialed first in a pilot project with a thorough evaluation of its effects before it is rolled out to the whole nation.

Elections and Ballot Papers: add an option on the ballot paper 'none of the above.' This offers frustrated voters a more differentiated expression of their will than to stay away from the election or to hand in an invalid ballot paper. It also allows a statistical evaluation of the percentage of the 'none of the above' votes.

Reintroduction of Freedom of Speech: abolish all laws that counteract freedom of speech or a clear distinction between intolerable incitement to commit crimes against persons on one side and politically uncomfortable reports and opinions on the other side. Objective criticism should always be welcome, especially when this is based on facts and logical argument-tation.

New Rules for Public Organizations: conversion of public sector accounting to a publicly accessible blockchain-based accounting system.

New Rules for Media: Reduction of the participation of parties in media companies to one which must clearly bear the party abbreviation in its name, e.g. "SPD Media." There should be a ban of ownership of media companies for persons or organizations involved in the production or trading of arms or other military material (ownership of at least 1%) and also a disclosure of the ownership structure of media companies above a certain range. The last beneficiaries have to be mentioned in the imprint from 5%.

New Rules for Public Media: Abolition of politics filling positions in public media institutions. All content has to be provided under a Creative Commons license. Restriction of the public-law bodies to a quality-assured basic supply of information. Introduction of a 'Consumer Control Council' at state and federal level, composed of non-party citizens elected by lot for four years. Advice to the Control Council by a citizen-elected honorary committee consisting of retired non-party journalists.

How should the extended program be determined?

The extended program is the second thematic layer for the new party. New topics can be added with a two-third or a three fourth majority. Unlike the core program, the extended program is more flexible and can add or drop topics more easily.

As I have written in my book *Upgrading Democracy*:[6]

> "You can compare the Proxy Party with a white canvas waiting to be painted. The canvas itself sets the frame with its form (democracy and transparency). The painter should wear clear glasses (media) so that he can judge his environment and the results of his work on the canvas as objectively as possible. The party members must agree on the theme of the picture, the materials used, and the atmosphere of the picture. They co-operatively design the work."

Discussions about topics to add should focus on shared values and common ground. The challenge is to find shared values and common ground in spite of political discussions majorly being shaped by discussions in different languages:[7]

- A progressive will communicate along the oppressor-oppressed axis
- A conservative will communicate along the civilization-barbarism axis
- A libertarian will communicate along the liberty-coercion axis

It is so easy to think of someone else as being politically crazy, stupid, biased, lazy or deceitful as 'he doesn't get what is really at stake.'

The Proxy Party is about all these schools of thought and some more, like the Democracy-Strengthening- Dismantling axis. It's not about moral superiority. It's not about demonizing the other side. It is about an appreciative discussion with the goal of finding solutions for our common challenges. This does not require agreement on all points, but only on some basic values that almost all of us share. In most cases, the participants of a discussion don't differ in the values themselves, but in their assessment of where society currently stands in achieving these values, the priorities of these values and how they should be achieved.

Since a 100% achievement of one of these basic values is hardly possible or requires a great deal of resources and affects other values, it is almost always a matter of weighing up how we want to achieve the optimum in achieving the common values. If we discuss on the basis of verifiable facts, logical conclusions, and a weighing up of these basic values, good solutions will emerge.

In order to achieve these solutions together, we must all be open and not simply fall back on the learned answers of our 'quick thinking'. We must follow a deliberate critical process in which we do not think as 'aggressive lawyer' but rather as 'impartial judge'.

As Hannah Arendt aptly pointed out, reality does not lie with one person, but between persons:

> "If someone wants to see and experience the world as it really is, he can do so by only understanding that it is something is shared with many people, lies between them, separates and links them, showing itself differently to each and comprehensible only to the extent that many people can talk about it and exchange their opinions and perspectives with one another over and against one another."
>
> -Hannah Arendt

You can compare the common search for truth with the addition of extra senses, which give the truth more sharpness through the addition of further perceptions:

- The second eye corrects the perceptions of the first and adds depth perception and peripheral vision
- An ear complements the perception with an echolocation

My suggested course of action for the extended program of the proxy party would be ..

> .. to renew all topics of the extended program at the end of the year and the annual member conference.
>
> .. to send each topic, which doesn't receive a 60% majority vote, into the official deliberation process described before and decided upon at the next annual member conference.

The Proxy Party offers benefits to dedicated individuals and groups with specific issues. Based on thorough preparation of their topic they have a good chance to be heard in the Proxy Party. This gives them a much better chance to make their concerns heard than by founding their own party, which has only a marginal chance of political representation.

My personal opinion what the Proxy Party should focus on in the extended program
While the core program focuses on democracy and transparency as a precondition of an honest and representative system, the extended program has to focus on

solutions to our pressing problems. Let me share what I proposed in my book *Upgrading Democracy* (with some minor changes):[8] In short, it is foreseeable that 'business as usual' continuing will lead to a catastrophe and that the changes proposed by most parties will not suffice while others bring us too close to an authoritarian regime.

The following is a list of what I consider to be the central and most urgent questions we as a society should ask ourselves and find solutions for:

- How do we provide billions of people with a livelihood and meaning if technological progress destroys far more jobs than it creates?
- How do we reduce poverty so that everyone can lead a dignified life?
- How do we raise money for the elderly with fewer workers and far more older people?
- How can we change the game to produce more winners and fewer losers, soften the fall of users and make people act kindlier and more fairly while playing the game?[9]
- How can we prepare for a global financial crisis?
- How can we prepare for a Euro crisis?
- How can we make a decisive contribution to improving the situation in developing countries quickly and sustainably, so that people no longer need to immigrate to Europe/the US in large numbers?
- How can we massively reduce environmental degradation?
- How can we prevent 'The New Cold War' from becoming hot?
- How can we modify our economic system to positively influence the above-mentioned points?
- How can we assure that we don't just "dream up the nicest fantasy and drift of a cliff in search for it but look at the real world, be strong enough to face it - and from there on, try to do what's best and most realistic given the circumstances?"[10]

List of the main underlying factors:

- Our economic and financial system
- Technological progress
- Environmental policy
- Demographic development: aging society
- Economic and development aid policy
- Societal development

- Geopolitics and foreign policy

Some approaches in the form of questions:

1. How can technological progress be used more effectively to achieve a significant improvement in the quality of life of all people, including those who are not in official employment or have already left the labor force, without weakening the entrepreneurial forces that generate these innovations?

2. How should an economic and monetary and societal system be designed so that as many people as possible experience a noticeable improvement in their quality of life? How can it be constructed more resilient?

3. How should fair trade be designed and how should it be complemented by an effective development aid policy so that the quality of life in developing countries can be significantly and sustainably improved?

4. How can an adapted or a new economic system and an environmental policy ensure a massive reduction in the depletion of resources and the accumulation of toxins, without limiting points factors one to three too much? How can technological innovations contribute to this?

5. How can we contribute to a de-escalation of the political situation with a new foreign policy?

6. How can we establish a 'learning political system' that focuses on well-balanced facts instead of political fiction and self-critically checks the results of its decisions and is open enough to change its course if required?

FINDING, PRIORITIZING AND VOTING ON TOPICS

The Proxy Party focuses on designing and securing party-internal information processes and democratic processes effectively and efficiently and implementing the results developed in the processes:

Important points of the content-related work are above all to:

- pick up new topics
- weight the incoming topics with the members
- prepare important topics
- enable factual input and fact-checking
- provide a platform for a deliberation process that aims at knowledge gain for all participants and their individual forming of their political will
- create a culture that focusses on finding common ground
- determine if the topics should be included in the party's Priority Program
- restrict reopening of topics already discussed in order to be able to advance thematically (a prerequisite for a re-introduction, i.e.: if decisive facts have changed and the majority is in favor of reopening or if a 2/3 majority opts to reopen the topic).

Detailed party rules should at least consider the following aspects sufficiently:

1. Input of topics by individual members on the basis of a two-page-template form ("Why is the topic important?") including a half-page abstract. These must receive a minimum number of votes (e.g. 60%) in a member preliminary vote of less than 1% randomly selected members (but at least 50 members). If a member

does not respond within a certain period of time, he will be replaced by an alternate member. Instead of a simple yes/no alternative, a different point system is used. Example: Five rating options "completely unimportant" (0%)/"not important" (25%)/"somehow important" (50%)/"important" (75%)/"very important" (100%). Potentially, the metric of importance can be split into two dimensions: 'importance' and 'urgency.'

A good preparation for the topic is very important. If the topic is well described and logically structured, many members will decide in favor of dealing with it and will proceed in the process. In order to reduce the expected flood of topics and increase their quality, a topic is not allowed to be submitted for voting without an initial preparation/ stage of maturity. If a member is not able to prepare the topic, he can search for and win other members for the preparation on the platform of the party.

In the founding and initial phase of the Proxy Party, it is advisable to focus on two core issues of the party: 'democracy' and 'transparency.' This can quickly create a well-coordinated and coherent basis on which the party can build for other topics.

2. The priorities for processing are determined by the approval rate of the topics. If a topic has 86% approval, then this is prioritized over a topic that reached only 82%. This, however, is relativized by the support of the party members. If the central resources are fully utilized and no volunteers work on the preparation of the topic, the 86% topic might get postponed while the 82% topic with more active members can take the next step.

3. Structured discussion of the topic, on the basis of standardized thematic decision templates. All papers should contain in-depth links. Factual claims such as numbers must include a reference to a trustworthy source. Whenever possible a link to the base data must be included. All participants taking part in the creation of the document must disclose in which way and how strongly they could be biased. All users that are able to change the document itself have to register and prove their expertise in the respective areas. At a later stage, different levels of discussion forums can be introduced for troll avoidance. Those would be 'read-only' for all members that don't have at least 10/100/1000 delegated votes on the respective topic. It also might be an interesting idea to split discussion vote delegation from actual voting delegation.[11]

The topic experts among party members are responsible for quality assurance. Everyone must be aware that a six-page presentation of a topic cannot fully reflect it. But even an 80% or 90% solution is far better than anything that today's policy achieves. The document will include:

> two-page introduction and facts
> one-page sketch of interdependent relationships (system thinking)
> one-page pro-argumentation
> one-page counter-argumentation incl. risks
> one-page recommendation (with different options) of the board of directors or the circle of experts on the basis of the party's fundamental values

The interdependencies are shown in a graphical representation which includes the most important factors and results. This illustrates how individual factors influence the outcome. The limitation to six pages should be a goal but will not always be achievable. This can lead to e.g. a counter-argumentation which is twice as long as the pro-argumentation.

4. During the actual deliberation in the forums with in-depth links, objective and solution-oriented discussions are held. Personal attacks, to be defined in a 'rule book", and other disturbing actions lead to temporary or permanent exclusion from the discussion of this topic. Above all, the rules have to focus on efficiency and a culture of mutual respect and the will to find common ground. Otherwise, this part of the thematic coordination will quickly degenerate into an unproductive shouting game and a lot of work. It can easily lead to a standstill. A potential cure for longwinded unhelpful posts would be to limit the number of words per discussion participant (online discussion) or time (face-to-face discussion). Each member is only allowed to write more if other participants mark her previous contributions as valuable, e.g. new facts introduced, new interdependency established. Contrary to Facebook, you don't 'like' a post but 'thank a participant for new insights'. By limiting the number of words and activating further contributions only after confirmed added value by other members, participants are forced to prepare a shorter, more precise wording that focuses on valuable new contributions.

5. Adaptation of the draft sketched under Point 3, based on the outcomes of the discussion.

6. Not all members will have interest or time to discuss or vote on all topics. Therefore, a 'topic-based delegate system' based on blockchain technology will be established (Liquid Democracy). Here, each party member can delegate his vote completely or for topic areas to another member or group of members. 24 hours before the election date, the election system sends the information on how the delegate vote is used, to the member. The voting delegation can be canceled by the member at any time. The vote on a topic can be overwritten with a personally cast vote at any time.

The vote asks whether the member has read the decision paper ('yes' or 'no'). It is also asking, whether the member's opinion was influenced by the preparatory paper in such a way that he voted differently than he would have done before reading the document. This is important for an evaluation of the percentage of readers and whether the paper has made a difference in their decisions.

7. Determination of the voting share of the party members and transfer to the elected representatives, e.g. 70% YES /20% NO/ 10% abstention = with 10 deputies seven vote for YES, two for NO, and one abstains.

Distribution of votes according to the preference of representatives. It should be achieved that as many deputies as possible can vote as they would vote on their own initiative. The obligation to vote differently in order to represent the voting weight of the party members as 1:1 as possible is minimized by the vote distribution system. The 'democratic burden' is evenly distributed.

8. It is recorded how the individual representatives of that party voted and reconciled with the system's inputs. The representatives should have voted in exactly the same way as was pre-determined by the weighting of party members and the allocation of the vote distribution system. In the case of roll-call votes, this is officially recorded. In the case of anonymous parliamentary votes, a way is to be found to uncover discrepancies. The party will try to influence parliament to ensure, that in principle, all thematic parliamentary votes are taken by name.

9. Transparent publication on the party's website:

- Party internal thematical decision papers based on templates (published before the vote)
- How each representative will vote (published before the vote)
- Comparison of the voting behavior of the party members (recorded via the blockchain) with the voting behavior of the representatives; consistency in

%.

- All documents are secured by a blockchain (timestamp).
- There is no external commentary function for the decision-papers in order not to slow down the party's work. 100% perfection can never be achieved on complex issues.

The published thematic decision papers can also be viewed externally. This leads to an increase in the competence of the members of parliament of other parties with regard to the topics and makes the rigid voting of this party as a block more difficult. Parties with a centralist organization could thus come under 'democratic pressure'. The thematic decision papers are also accessible to citizens. They too can use the well-balanced preparatory papers to read up on the subject briefly and informatively.

Of course, votes of the Proxy Party in parliament could also be allocated more traditionally, as a bloc. The important difference to the normal party: The instruction for the vote would not come from the party leadership, but from the party base. But this traditional procedure would still override many voices by condensing the votes to one unison decision. Therefore, bloc voting is an inferior solution of representation.

PART II

CHALLENGES AND OUTLINE OF A SOLUTION

GOING BEYOND 'SIMPLE' DIRECT DEMOCRACY

The benefits of the Proxy Party approach are quite obvious. The direct results are massive improvements in the quality of representation of the citizens and the reduction of corruption:

Better representation
The greatest benefit of the grassroot democratic approach lies in the far better representation:

- The members are in the driving seat to decide what topics should be tackled.
- The members are empowered to directly participate in the stages of fact gathering and deliberation.
- The members can take on the decision and decide about the best solution themselves.
- The members and their decisions are represented 1:1 in parliament.

Less corruption
It is far harder to convince many hundred thousand party members than a few hundred elected representatives and their staff. There are simply not enough favors to give to all the party members by lobbyists.

The connection between the size of the group to be influenced and corruption is explained in the book *The Dictators Handbook*. As the size of the group grows, so does the level of corruption shrink.[12] In other words, the introduction of direct democracy would be the optimal strategy against corruption. Another more entertaining way to learn about the topic is a 20-minute video titled *"The Rules for Rulers."*

The difference to the old model of political parties and the working and results of the grassroot democratic approach of the Proxy Party can be sketched as follows:

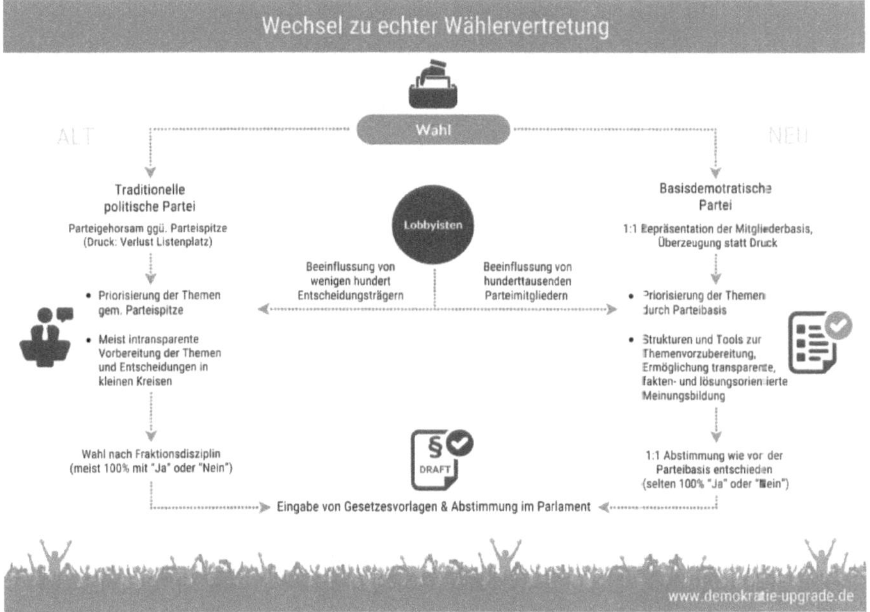

Additional ingredients for a successful Proxy Party

Challenges that affect every democratic system naturally also apply to a grassroots democratic party. By effectively addressing the following challenges, the proxy party can become the most reliable, transparent and honest party ever:

INEFFECTIVENESS. The party might not be effective to represent its members if special interest groups try to take over the party to drive their specific agenda or 'suck up too much political energy.' It will not be effective if it fails to collect well-balanced facts and ensure neutral facilitation of the formation of a political will result in the decision.

INEFFICIENCY. The direct democratic approach is not efficient, as discussing everything with every member is very time consuming and nearly endless. Even if a consensus is reached with the existing members, new members will want to reopen topics and discuss them again. It will not be efficient when loud voices with very articulate opinions drown gentler voices with facts and knowledge.

DECISION MANIPULATION. The decisions of the members can be heavily influenced by those that (a) select the specialists the data is sourced from, (b) gather the facts, (c) prepare the decision paper, and (d) facilitate the deliberation process. Therefore, the Proxy Party needs safeguarded information and democratic processes.

MEDIA. As we haven't encountered many topics personally, we form pictures of the outside world based on external information. This plays a decisive role in the decisions of the parties' members. Most of us get informed by mainstream media, far fewer from alternative media. Some use social networks as a filter to be informed about the relevant news. Evermore often, we end up in separate realities[13] that make it hard to agree on anything.

TECH MANIPULATION. Democracy initiatives worldwide are very skeptical regarding electronic voting systems, and rightly so. In the case of centralized systems, there is a serious risk that they could be hacked. To prevent this, blockchain-based decentralized systems must be used. Manipulation when entering new data (e.g. a vote) into the system must also be prevented. On the other side, the systems need to be easily used so that the hurdle for users is as low as possible to inform themselves, take part in the deliberation process, and vote.

The rest of this short book tries to find approaches to tackle the above-mentioned weaknesses and enlarge the chance for a direct democratic party to be successful.

EFFICIENT UND EFFECTIVE

A grassroots democratic political party is not an end in itself. Its main purpose is to act on behalf of its members and to bring about political decisions in their interests. To be successful in this endeavor, it has to be effective (doing the right things) and efficient (doing the things right).

An effective Proxy Party

I argue that a Proxy Party is more effective than conventional political parties if it:

> (a) represents its members and the voters better than the current political parties and

> (b) collects balanced and easily comprehensible facts so that the individual effort for additional fact-checks is reduced when forming an opinion. On this basis, an independent decision-making process of its members and thus also well-considered decisions are made possible.

REPRESENTATION

The grassroot democratic Proxy Party will aim at a 1:1 representation of its members by transferring the party's internal votes to parliament. It enables its members to propose topics, rank them, take topics in their own hands and decide about them themselves:

- By allowing its members to bring in topics and rank them it focusses on the topics important for its members.
- By allowing its members to decide on their own it will reveal the true voting ratios of the members.

- By not forcing a decision to one side but simply representing the voting ratios it will represent the true will of its members.

GATHERING WELL BALANCED FACTS AND NEUTRAL FACILITATION

Anyone who has ever dealt with the strengths and weaknesses of our thinking knows that we humans have two kinds of thinking. This is described by the Nobel Prize winner for economics, Daniel Kahneman, in his book *Thinking, Fast and Slow*.

The book states, during evolution, humans developed a strategy in which most of the decisions of the day are made without much thinking. We just use proven shortcuts. This 'fast-thinking,' is however very susceptible and is subject to many cognitive biases that can be used for manipulation. In political decision-making, the most important thing is not to let the voter decide 'from the gut.' Instead, he must know the facts and be motivated to deal with them. He should be motivated to 'think slow' and will then have a good basis for his decision.

In doing so, the Proxy Party relies on science in the sense of a quotation from Dieter Nuhr, German comedian, to determine the facts:

> "Knowledge does not mean that you are 100% sure, but that you have enough facts to have a well-founded opinion. Because many people are offended when scientists change their mind: No, no! That is normal! Science is just THAT the opinion changes when the facts change. Because science is not a doctrine of salvation, not a religion that proclaims absolute truths. And those who constantly shout, 'Follow science!' have obviously not understood this. Science does not know everything, but it is the only reasonable knowledge base we have. That is why it is so important."

The Proxy Party is a neutral facilitator for the forming of the political will of its members and all citizens. It tries to enable well-informed decisions by providing relevant, well-balanced, checked data and provide systems and an environment in which respectful deliberation with a focus on common ground can take place.

Instead of manipulating its members and all citizens with very one-sided selected facts, misleading statistics, etc., it will simply show the situation as it is, as well-balanced as possible, and let its members decide on their own. The Proxy Party will enable its members to find their educated will and thus will far better represent its members than any existing party.

An efficient Proxy Party

Being theoretically effective doesn't help when the Proxy Party is majorly occupied with itself like many other grassroot democratic organizations. It also has to focus on efficiency. In the end, it will be judged by its achievements and not by its potential and lofty goals.

Therefore, it is important to agree on rules that will enable the party's officials and representatives to act efficiently on behalf of its members without sacrificing the effectiveness of representation.

THINGS THE MEMBERS SHOULD DIRECTLY VOTE ON

I see two things the members should definitely vote on directly:

- The Party Program (Core Program and Extended Program)
- The Representatives (internal: party officials; elections: direct candidates, list candidates and their order on the list)

The party program is the most fundamental building block to decide. It should be decided on by all members. It sets common values and ensures common goals. This is the only decision that the members have to take themselves and can't delegate.

The election of party internal posts has to be also voted on by its members. Here I see a delegation of votes as a good option as members who have personally met certain candidates will have a better base for a good decision.

The election of candidates on city, district, regional, state, and county levels has to be also voted on by its local members. This determines the direct candidates as well as the list candidates and their positions on the party list. Here I also see a delegation of votes as a good option.

In the election of persons, a ranking procedure should be followed, in which the voter arranges the candidates in the order of his preference ('ranked-choice voting'). The candidate with the fewest points is eliminated and his share of the vote is distributed among the second candidates of the voters who voted for him as first candidate, etc.

A simple YES/NO-vote should be replaced by a more sophisticated vote for each candidate. Alternatively, you could provide the following scale for each candidate/ solution: strong rejection/rejection/neutral/approval/strong approval) with the values -3/-1/0/+1/+3. The winner/ winning solution will be determined by adding up the total number of points.

For all 'officials' of the proxy party, e.g. board of directors or spokesperson, a proxy party internal survey is conducted every two months. Here two values are asked:

1. "Does XYZ represent the ideals of the party (democracy, transparency, 1:1 representation)?"
2. "Has XYZ harmed the party with his actions?"

For the answer to the first question the following answers can be selected: very negative/ negative/ neutral/ positive/ very positive) with the values -3/ -1/ 0/ +1 / +3. For the answer to the second question the following answers can be selected: has done much harm/ has done harm/ neutral/ has not done harm. If the first value falls below zero, a survey is automatically started, asking all members whether the official should still remain in office. If the second value rises above one, then such a poll is also triggered.

5% TAKE OVER VOTE AND LIQUID DEMOCRACY

It is obvious: If the party insists that all members take all decisions at the member base, it will fail. By trying this approach, the active members will be overloaded and will eventually burn out and decisions will be taken too late or will be ill-prepared. Most likely, this approach will achieve all of these results.

My suggestion would be to combine the best of both worlds:

a. Party bodies, officials and spokespersons of the party who are able to act independently on the basis of a clearly defined, concrete party program
b. A 'democracy by exception' approach with a qualifying 5% hurdle. In this way, the higher effort for a member vote is reduced to those cases in which this is necessary or desired or required by the statutes.

The party officials would be guided by the descriptive party program. If the candidates are picked correctly and guided by a well-written program, they could decide on their own on how to vote in parliament. They would act like normal representatives.

However, the representatives would have to announce their voting decision to the members in time to give them a chance to interfere. All members are allowed to initiate a 'takeover vote' that, if successful, would take the decision out of the hands of the representatives and in the hands of the members and initiate the official fact gathering and deliberation process at the member level. The takeover vote needs to pass a qualifying 5% of all members incl. delegated votes (see below 'liquid democracy').

The concept of 'liquid democracy' allows for the flexible, short-term and topic-specific transfer of votes ('delegated votes') to a person/group who/that is believed to have expertise on a topic or a similar attitude to one's own and is therefore suitable to represent the voter.

The specialist committees also have the right to kick-off decisions taken at the member basis without a take-over vote by the members. This could be relevant if there is any doubt as to whether a sufficiently secured decision can be made.

In both cases, the importance of these topics (and the time to be spent on them) will be determined by the members and the qualified volunteer power for the preparation of these topics.

The proposed system would be very flexible:

- Guided by the core program and the extended program, representatives should be able to take independent decisions on the issues defined in the program. The members will get pre-informed about the vote of their representatives. If 5% of the members believe that the representatives misinterpret these guidelines, they can obtain a member vote on the specific topic.

- For issues brought to Parliament by other parties, that are not included in the party program, representatives should announce their voting preference to the party members in advance. They should connect with each other and give the members reasons for their vote in writing. In parallel, they should ask for a supplementary assessment from topic specialists.

- Voting at the party base level should be primarily used to prepare the party's own legislative initiatives.

- All topics that appeal to the members can be prepared at member level, for example by a randomly selected specialist group, if sufficient members can be found for the qualified preparation.

TOPIC PREPARATION AND FOCUS

Topics that have not yet been prepared pose a challenge. For these, there is not yet a sound basis for a decision that would enable the members to prepare themselves quickly and well balanced. A distinction must be made here:

- The quality of active submissions of topics to the parliament must be guaranteed. The active submission can only take place when the decision basis has reached a high degree of maturity and the majority of the basis decides in favor of a proposal.

- The hurdle can be lowered when voting on laws and topics introduced by other parties. If the preparation time is too short or if the wording of draft legislation is misleading or artificially complicated, there should be a tendency to reject the proposal, if only to point out a lack of democracy. However, the basis can also simply rely on its representatives who, guided by the party program, will vote according to their consciences.

Not every topic is equally important. Especially at the beginning, a not clear-cut thematic focus leads to a dilution of the focus and the profile of the party. This would lead to a decrease in the quality of the work. If the party develops the ambition to work on far more topics, then it will be important to attract many specialists and active members to prepare and discuss these topics, slowly increasing the number and the breadth of topics covered by the party.

It may be that the 5% approach to the takeover vote of the members is too high or too low. If it is chosen too low, it can lead to a flood of votes and thus to an overload of members. If it is set too high, too many approaches fail to carry out topic voting at the member level. Therefore, a paragraph should be established in the party's statutes which stipulates that the level of the 5% percentage hurdle must be voted on every six months. This can be done within the framework of a permanent general meeting. All the members can regularly consider whether the party officials and the members use their rights wisely or whether this percentage should be amended.

FACTS VS. OPINION

The Proxy Party might not be effective when loud voices with very articulate opinions drown gentler voices with facts and knowledge. It is also counterproductive to start discussions before having facts. It is especially counterproductive if certain facts are not allowed to be mentioned as it would be 'politically incorrect.'

> "Political correctness is fascism pretending to be manners."
> - George Carlin

This is, of course, somewhat pointed, but it is at least 80% true since most of the current exaggerations do not allow for differentiation and are not accessible to logical arguments. Solutions must take precedence over sensitivities. Blocking facts mostly results in blocking potential solutions.

The party needs to find a way to attract experts to join the party or at least support the party with their knowledge in the fact-finding and deliberation phase.

SAFEGUARDED INFORMATION AND DECISION PROCESSES

A democracy without deliberation (based on well-balanced facts) is a weak democracy.

Focusing on political differences while demonizing the other side makes a democracy very vulnerable to a divide and conquer strategy. It misses out chances to agree on common goals and put forward measures that a great majority of citizens would vote for.

> "The point with democracy isn't that the majority is always right. The point is that there is a process of free and sufficiently systemized truth-seeking and dialogue going on for small groups to be able to prove the rest of us wrong, again and again, so that values, opinions and laws can evolve and adapt."[14]
>
> - Hanzi Freinacht, Nordic Ideology

Bringing in Facts and Checking Them

The focus on well-balanced information as input for the deliberation and decision process will be one of the main challenges of the new party (see the chapter about media):

- When is a fact a fact and worthy to be included in the discussion? Definition of the gold standard e.g. original data gathered, tested and peer-reviewed facts. Who paid for the evaluation (and thus sets the tone)?

- How does the party deal with factual input and check its validity? How does it value the input of a lobby organization? Effort to check versus proven validity of the facts.

A wise strategy would be to attract retired experts who are interested in politics and no longer need a job to support them. They have a lot of knowledge in their field and are able to speak freely. After all, they don't have to fear to ruin their career or losing their job for speaking up.

Facilitation Process

The facilitation process should not be rushed. There should be set time minimums as rushed decisions have a higher risk to end up as bad decisions. A good process involves 'slow thinking' and deliberation as much as possible as 'fast thinking' is too vulnerable to external influence misleading the understanding and the decision. It takes time to ..

- .. gather facts and check them
- .. understand the context and the interdependencies
- .. go in the deliberation process

The facilitators have to be well trained. They have to be as neutral as possible to the decision itself. They must be only interested in adhering to the process to enable a truly educated decision of the participants. They should also be trained to evaluate the process itself and propose improvements to it.

An interesting facilitation idea might be to pass around a 'talking stick' and institutionalize a first task to describe the position of the previous speaker. This would lead to a higher focus to understand the other participant and should result in a better deliberation process.

An idea to measure the effectiveness of the deliberation process would be to have an in-poll and an out-poll. The difference and shifts in political opinions would indicate how effective the deliberation process was in changing minds. Another idea would be to measure the increase of the ability of the party's members to discourse over time, an important precondition for a good deliberation process.

Decision Paper

The decision paper is sent out to all members with the request to post their votes. It is not meant to be a full replacement of taking part in the deliberation process but at least delivers its essence to the members who had no time to take part in the process itself. I propose to have two pages for a description of the problem, two pages for pro and contra argumentation, one page for a system chart with interdependencies and one page as conclusion.

I am aware that the limitation to six pages will not work for every topic. However, an extension should only be made if it is absolutely necessary, because it will also reduce the number of members who read the paper in the first place.

This decision paper is not to be mixed up with the preparatory text for legislative proposals. This is often (a) far too long, (b) not understandable enough, (c) not well balanced, (d) not descriptive in its resulting consequences, and (e) not embedded in the larger context. Posting only this as a decision basis would result in frustration and many votes based on the well-sounding wording of the initiative instead of its content.

One fact to bear in mind is that a decision paper or a discussion will never be able to describe the problem in its full complexity and fully evaluate the potential solutions and their estimated outcomes: getting closer to a 100% description of the complex challenge versus length of the decision paper and time to be invested to create and read it.

Voting on Topics

Another important problem to tackle is to ensure that behind each member is a real human and that each human only has one registration as a member (and just one vote). This is easier when you meet the new member in person and take a look at her Identity Card and note down the ID-number. A member registration via digital registration with an e-mail must be supplemented by further details and checks.

The party will have to decide about its voting procedures. There are multiple options:

Does it adhere to the normal policy of 'one person - one vote' or does it give experts more weight than regular members? After all, you shouldn't ask the regular guy how to build a save bridge, but an engineer specialized in building bridges. But how does a member prove its expertise in a field? Can this expertise be earned while taking part in the grassroot democratic process of the Proxy Party? Should the Proxy Party give its members a certain amount of voting points each month which they can freely spend on the topics that really interest them? Should these points count 1:1 or should they count as proposed in the 'quadratic voting' approach (1 vote = 1 point, 2 votes = 4 points, 3 votes = 9 points, etc.)? So, if you want to give your full 50 points to one decision that really speaks to you, these will just count for seven votes. Or should voting points decay over time so that a vocal minority would have less power?

This quadratic voting allows the strength of the voter's point of view to be expressed and it is very costly to dominate a vote. People committed to a topic are generally also more interested in it; they are better informed about it. So, this voting procedure should also lead to better results in purely factual terms.

Another alternative is the Australian Flux Party's issue-based direct democracy system. This is based on a market model for votes and aims to determine the best policy decentrally.[15]

It would be wise to only vote on something that you truly understand. So, it would be wise to delegate your vote on topics you don't understand to someone you trust with this topic. But how do you know whom to trust in this field when you haven't got the slightest idea what they are talking about? And: Of cause, those people that really should delegate their votes wouldn't even recognize they should (Dunning-Kruger effect).

Celebrities within the party might amass many votes and thus influence the party's decision unduly. In case you opted for the 'quadratic voting' approach described above, even if 2,500 members give a celebrity 1 vote each, the vote of the celebrity with her delegated votes would only count as 50 votes.

Media

A general problem within democratic societies is that the population can easily be influenced by the media. If this provides a distorted view of the actual situation and its meaning, the decisions of the influence can be highly distorted.

It is therefore very important that a direct-democratic party succeeds in shedding light on this darkness of 'opinion making' through the systematic and always comprehensible provision of trustworthy bases for decision-making.

It should be borne in mind that even if the party succeeds in aggregating all the relevant data, reviewing it and producing a balanced decision paper, most members will still decide mainly on the basis of the media input they consume.

THE IDEAL OF POLITICAL MEDIA

Concerning the political realm press/media is the fourth political power and can be described as a kind of 'early warning system and security net of democracy.' If the controls and security systems of the political system itself fail, the media can expose the deficits and alert the public.

The media should critically scrutinize the policies of parliament and the government to uncover issues that policymakers would like to keep secret, especially when they act questionably or try to circumvent democratic processes altogether. The media should show backgrounds and embed the latest news in them. Facts and opinions are clearly to be separated. Media should enable citizens to form their own picture and make informed decisions.

The job of a political journalist is not that of the stenographer. His job is rather to inform the public about what influential people and institutions do with their money and on their behalf.

Of cause, it is easier to act as a stenographer and write along with overnment narratives. It is easier as you don't have to think much about it and as a bonus get more interviews or perhaps even an exclusive once in a while.

> "Journalism is printing what someone else does not want printed.
> Everything else is public relations."
> -George Orwell

THE DANGEROUS REALITY

The reality in many countries, however, is different and the media is far too close to the government. Some of the media are even controlled directly by parties. Most important media outlets are in the hands of a few wealthy individuals.

This leaves power in the hands of a few to manipulate the rest of us. These individuals don't have to make money from their ownership of the media; they can simply see it as 'a cost center like a PR department' to drive their agenda and make up the invested money somewhere else.

A different approach with publicly financed broadcasting institutions seems to have mostly failed mainly because of a lack of critical oversight. Their very reason to exist as a state-funded entity is to provide well-balanced high-quality information to help citizens in forming their political will contributing to a functioning democracy.

In reality, true independence was rarely achieved by any of these broadcasting mediums. Instead of being a critical observer and commentator, they far too often ended up as cheerleaders for government politics.

For alternative and social media, governments make sure that disseminating so-called 'fake news' can lead to severe punishment. In Hungary, a journalist can be sentenced for up to five years in prison.[16] Romania, Bulgaria, Russia, and Belarus go in the same direction and some European governments have moved to restrict media access to 'authorized' COVID-related information.[17]

> "The best way to combat disinformation is to let independent media do their job and to guarantee journalists' access to decision-makers and information related to the crisis. Instead, governments across central and eastern Europe are hindering the press's ability to inform the public about the virus and are equipping themselves with laws that can be used to quash scrutiny."[18]
> -Scott Griffen, IPI Deputy Director

IS IT REALLY SO EASY TO MANIPULATE US?

We are continually bombarded with millions of impressions. Only a few can be consciously processed by our brains. Our brain chooses shortcuts as it doesn't want to be unnecessarily burdened. These shortcuts are controlled by stereotypes or 'pictures' that help us to make fast 'standard decisions.'

In our complex world, we develop images of people and things we have never encountered personally in life. These are largely taken from the media. By consuming the same media, these images are consolidated through repetition and form the basis of our decisions and actions. Media does not solely describe reality but (at least partly) creates it.

NO SUCH THING AS ABSOLUTE OBJECTIVITY

On the other side, there is no such thing as absolute objective journalism. Journalists always have to pick the parts they want to feature and thus select.

SYSTEM CRITICISM OF THE MEDIA

According to Professor Rainer Mausfeld, the entire media system "is structured economically and organizationally in such a way that it does not require any targeted personal control. Its conformity to the prevailing ideology already results from filter mechanisms that are a direct consequence of the structural economic power relations in which the media are embedded."[19]

David Goeßmann also doesn't see a conscious manipulation as the core problem: "In principle, journalists from media companies and broadcasters report what they have in front of their eyes, quite professionally and objectively. They do not do this in a vacuum, but within a very narrow ideological framework. As stated before, the media have an institutional side. This list works like a set of filters through which information and opinions pass. And these filters are designed so that not all information, opinions, backgrounds and voices have the same chance to pass. They don't receive the same attention - even if their relevance is essential for understanding events."[20]

Noam Chomsky describes a process of socialization for journalists that are only allowed to write what they want, as they have proven long ago that nobody has to tell them what to write.

The results of the other side of the medal, when young journalists don't follow this line, are expressed in the resignation letter of the journalist Bari Weiss to the New York Times:[21]

> "Rule One: Speak your mind at your own peril. Rule Two: Never risk commissioning a story that goes against the narrative. Rule Three: Never believe an editor or publisher who urges you to go against the grain. Eventually, the publisher will cave to the mob, the editor will get fired or reassigned, and you'll be hung out to dry."

SOME GENERAL THOUGHTS ON THE INFLUENCE OF THE MEDIA

A larger part of the media doesn't inform people objectively so that they can form their own view. Instead, most media try to form the opinion by spreading their 'pictures.' The rules of journalism geared towards neutrality are increasingly being abandoned in favor of a journalism with an educational mission. Basic journalistic standards are put on the back burner in order to be on the 'right side'.

> "Truth isn't a process of collective discovery, but an orthodoxy already known to an enlightened few whose job is to inform everyone else."
> -Bari Weiss, US Journalist

Complex topics are unilaterally defined by the framing set by the media reports and predefined terms and pictures. A judgmental ethic attempts to limit the field of discussion and prevent discussions about facts and opinions that go beyond the defined field. Urgently necessary discussions are prevented.

INSTRUMENTS OF MEDIA

Repetition. As marketing teaches us: the key is repetition. "Experimental studies show that an assertion made by the experimenters increases in the perceived truth of the observers the more frequently they are presented. This is even true if the experimenter explicitly declared them false before the experiment. We are unable to fight it. Even if you clarify the phenomenon beforehand with the test subject, it does not change the effect: the more often you hear an opinion, the more the perceived truth increases."[22]

Fast thinking and emotions instead of slow thinking and facts. According to Noam Chomsky, the propagandist does not want to convince, but to influence the emotions and behavior of people. He wants to frighten them, make them angry. He gives promises to them. Propaganda tries to replace self-sovereign thinking with the gut feeling of 'being right' with the accepted opinion.

Set and hide topics. If the mainstream media only reports on allowed topics, other topics are not public. Only a few politically interested individuals obtain additional information via alternative media.

Set terms and their interpretation. The race for the mind of the public is already won at an early stage by setting the frame and asking questions. If you accept the question, you are already in the construct of the person posing the questions. Topics can be very unilaterally defined by deliberately chosen one-sided terms spread via media. If you are able to define the terms, you have already gained half of the authority to interpret the topic. The choice of words directs the thoughts that arise when the word is pronounced:

- anti-corona protest vs. pro constitutional rights protests
- warn vs. threaten
- freedom fighter vs. terrorist
- resistance vs. terror
- peace mission vs. war
- military strike vs. war of aggression

Selective reporting. Selective reporting skips listing important facts that are relevant for assessing the situation. It only selects the facts that match its own agenda.

- Reporting on the Ukraine conflict and the image of the 'evil Russian'. Facts left out: the expansion of NATO as a threat to Russia, Crimea as former part of Russia given as a present to Ukraine, heavy investment of US in regime change, the background of the seizure of power in Ukraine and shots on police and civilians on the Maidan.
- Today's coverage of Venezuela is also very one-sided and international opinion much less unanimous than reported by the main media outlets.[23]
- The reports on the current corona epidemic are anything but balanced. The limitation to very few experts and the suppression of a broader scientific discussion has mainly led to an increase in the anxiety of the population. A fact-based weighing of the response of governments has failed to materialize.

The media do not lie - they shorten, hide, distort and tamper. But this is not a conscious act. It rather is a mix of their own perception of an increasingly complex reality and official political positions. "In order to avoid contradictions, they resort to the means of shortening - not least because they believe that this shortening facilitates the understanding of the public."[24]

Stephen Hebel adds: "They do not invent the 'good might stories' but they pass them on. The inventors are located elsewhere: in business associations, in the policy and PR departments of political parties, in foundations ... or in more or less covert propaganda departments ..."[25]

Selection of experts. A positive selection for government conform experts helps a lot to receive favorable expert advice supporting your point of view.

Discrediting Persons. A particularly perfidious way of combating other opinions is to socially stigmatize, exclude and defame opponents. They are given names like 'conspiracy nut or 'Nazi' or 'unpatriotic'. In extreme cases, this can take on a totalitarian character and end up in a career- and even life-threatening character assassination. Anyone who talks to these excluded people or even admits having read an article of them is then at least suspect, if not partly guilty ('guilt by association').

Hate Speech. The 'Hate Speech Laws' of many countries are dangerous to democracy itself. While true democracy lives from free speech and an open exchange of ideas, 'hate speech' allows for a rather arbitrary suppression of unwanted publicly expressed opinions. A vague definition of 'hate speech' not actually caring for facts but for the 'feeling of hate' is an excellent weapon for authoritarian governments.

"Once the premise is accepted that the state must censor public debate through the coercive criminal law, there is no logical stopping point, and the state will become empowered to prohibit the expression of an idea simply because the state, or society, finds that idea offensive or insulting. If real progress in human rights is to be made, such a future must be averted. As the Colombian delegate warned the General Assembly of the United Nations nearly half a century ago, 'to penalize ideas, whatever their nature, is to pave the way for tyranny.'"[26]

Something built to stop 'hate speech' will stop political dissidents next.

Opinion Polls. Opinion polls have the nimbus of taking the pulse of the street. But they can be easily manipulated (see: 'Statistics').

Statistics. "Never trust a statistic you didn't forge yourself." They can be manipulated by (a) the selection of the participants, (b) the questions and their wording including misleading usage of words and changes of definition over time, (c) the data representation with graphics and many more tricks. You should be very careful to trust your first impression. Definitely take a look at the entity funding the data collection or the work of the statisticians: Might this entity be interested in a certain outcome with a certain message?

Citing experts and research. Ask two experts and you will get three opinions. Why not only cite those that agree with your point of view? And surely you will have an easier time finding those when the research itself is dependent on third party financing. As the saying goes: "He who pays the piper calls the tune."

Talk Shows. Even if a real expert from the 'other side' is invited, he is only a single participant in the round for the opposing view. Often, he can only give his intro statement, has a few minutes in the middle, and his closing statement. The topic of discussion is rarely embedded in a larger context. The underlying mechanisms are only touched upon and solutions are only described superficially.

In short: the talk show only pretends to present and discuss a topic. The scope of the discussion, however, is set so that the topic must stay on the surface. What remains is a confused citizen who only knows that the subject is complicated and tedious. This suggests that he would be better off to leave this topic to the professionals, the politicians.

Psychology Behind the shrinking Diversity of Opinions Through Political Correctness. "...They are not simply offered information. Rather, the information is linked to certain opinions that one should have about certain information. And these opinions now are linked to moral evaluations. So that if they do not represent certain opinions themselves, they automatically stand in the corner of evil...And that's exactly how the attitude journalism is formed, which scandalizes any dissenting opinion, and which also makes clear to everyone the price one has to pay if one wants to be non-conformist, if one wants to express a dissenting opinion. This price is getting higher and higher."[27]

The US-lawyer and Vice President of the Mackinac Center for Public Policy, Joseph P. Overton, designed the following scale (Overton Window):

> current policy <=> popular view <=> reasonable <=> acceptable <=> radical <=> unthinkable

"The formal freedom to say what you think does not mean much if you no longer dare to think what you are not allowed to say. Since in the long run it's too exhausting to think differently than you talk, most people think politically correct or at least a lot of people do. What does that actually mean? We are not actually afraid of having a wrong opinion, but we are afraid of standing alone with our opinion. That is what social psychologists call fear of isolation. And this fear of isolation governs our world. But those who fear the anger of others easily agree with the opinion of the clear majority, even if they actually know better. You silence yourself. That is the censorship that really counts...You silence yourself in order not to jeopardize your good reputation."[28]

"You repeat what you say. And what you say is not the opinion of the majority, but the opinion of well-articulated minorities. This is the starting point for a dynamic, which Elisabeth Nölle-Neumann analyzed many decades ago and which she gave the name 'spiral of silence'. And exactly this spiral of silence is used today by political correctness. ... Because minorities are often well articulated, and because they find resonance in the echo of the mass media, individuals believe that they are themselves in the minority and the others are the majority. And that is why they remain silent. So, they fall silent because they believe themselves to be in the minority, perhaps even as a radical minority. They think that the others are in the majority. But those are simply well articulated and have the loudspeakers of the mass media on their side. In the end this mechanism leads to minority rule; democracy is not the rule of the majorities, but the rule of well-articulated minorities."[29]

Prof. Bolz criticizes the so-called intellectuals: "Their power-protected, sentimental, moralizing discourse of political correctness uses ethics as a means of justification and puts any dissident in the media pillory. The realm of the mind today falls apart into the self-righteous and the intimidated."[30]

The tools:

- Moralism (moralization makes discussion impossible and splits into good and evil)
- Language hygiene (politically correct language)
- Lazaret poetry (show pictures of crying, suffering children; only monsters have a different opinion)

Prof. Bolz considers the use of the mechanisms mentioned above to be very dangerous: "The greatest danger for democracy is not the hatred of the radical losers, but the silence of the many who feel patronized by the paternalism of the media elite."[31]

Social Media - The Echo Chamber. The algorithms of social media platforms serve their users' personalized information. They aim to keep them on their platform and earn more money from advertisers.

The user wanders in a self-created and algorithm created filter bubble, which deepens his own views and hides other ideas and world views. The algorithms of the platforms appeal to our human instincts. It will feed "…us a constant stream of increasingly more extreme and inflammatory content."[32] The platforms strengthen the bond with your tribe by sharing narrative confirmation. "The most snappily worded and convincingly argued receive the biggest rewards when they're shared, which then incentivizes others to share them too."[33] Anybody interested in the psychology of political tribes should read the detailed article *"Political Disney World"* by waitbutwhy.com.

If the user stumbles upon other ideas, they seem even more incomprehensible or even threatening. One of the reactions is 'hate speech.' The use of classic social media reinforces the further polarization of society.[34] Individuals are rather oriented along with identity politics, build their own tribes, focus on differences and miss to align along with common interests.

In the future, the situation is more likely to worsen. 'Deep Fakes' can be used to simulate realities that never existed.[35] Imagine what a deceptively genuine, but fake video of a politician could cause. Slander and manipulation become easier. It will also become easier to deny statements actually made as 'deep fake.'[36] A phenomenon that law professors Robert Chesney and Danielle Citron described as 'liar's dividend.'

1:1 TRANSFER TO PARLIAMENT

In rare cases, the political leadership of a typical party doesn't decide on its own but hands the vote to the member base, the majority will decide about the voting behavior of their representatives in parliament. Even if 49% of the members vote against a petition, all their representatives will still vote for it. This might even increase well above 50% when the party leader insists and threatens to resign if the party doesn't vote accordingly.

One major reason why the command style works well is the re-election process for the representatives. This is heavily dependent on the good-will of the party leaders influencing or even directly deciding about the list position of the candidate in the next election.

In my opinion, this process misses the point of democracy itself. Democracy has to represent the people and not their political parties. Artificially aggregating the will of its members at the intermediate step of a party to a 100% YES/NO-vote results in a loss of information and distortion of the political will and makes the party more vulnerable to corruption.

Members of political parties are individuals with individual minds and will not agree on all political issues. This is only possible in a 'one topic party' e.g. one aiming to install a Universal Basic Income (UBI). If you talk to these guys, you will see that even this group with a very narrow focus doesn't agree on how a UBI should look like.

The Proxy Party should aim to represent the will of its members as well as it can. If 80% of its members vote YES and 20% with NO, eight of 10 representatives should vote for YES in parliament and two with NO.

Some drawbacks would be:

- In many cases, the party wouldn't vote uniformly which will be interpreted as a dissonance by its critics.
- It would be hard to form a coalition with another party that is used to the artificial 100% consent voting. The party program of the Proxy Party offers very concrete cornerstones for negotiations but will not cover all areas. Finding a consensus on even a few additional points would probably take several months of intensive work.

But would it be so hard to communicate again and again that the aim of the party is not to vote against the will of a sizable part of the members but truly represent all of them? But would it be so hard to tell the coalition partner that just the projects that convince your member base will get their consent? Sure, a decision from the top is easier, but surely not more democratic.

PART III

QUESTIONS AND ANSWERS AND A CALL TO ACTION

QUESTIONS AND ANSWERS

How does the Proxy Party differ from a normal party?
The Proxy Party:

...is organized on the basis of grassroots democracy and also includes the most important right of the member of parliament (the voting right).

...obliges the elected representative to vote as determined by the party base.

...does not ignore the dissenting votes of its members but reflects their will in the vote.

...is, therefore, more relaxed in the internal discussion, since it is not a question of necessarily having to achieve a 50% majority.

...can function like a normal party if all members delegate their votes to the party leadership but has a 'grassroots democratic corrective.' The member can 'take back' the vote at any time, i.e. cancel the vote delegation to the party leadership. The members can then exercise each vote itself or transfer it to party members outside the party leadership circle.

...is focused on safeguarding the democratic processes and information processes within the party.

...will check facts or at least evaluate their basis.

...approaches a topic without ideological blinders.

...is focused on finding common ground and developing concrete, effective, and sustainable solutions.

...is focused on the internal discussion and the increase in knowledge for the participants.

...uses thematic summaries to inform everyone well-balanced about the most important facets of a subject area.

...is transparent and committed to extending this transparency to the entire political arena and all public institutions.

... is the 'democratic champion' in parliament and is relentlessly committed to the further development of democracy and the strengthening of its institutions.

But this is not a direct democracy, because only the party members are allowed to participate

The next stage of the democracy upgrade, the creation of a proxy party to represent its members, does not yet include the general introduction of direct democracy. Only the members of the party can have a say in how their representatives vote. Apart from the members, only experts are invited to give input on individual issues.

However, the proxy party will work to ensure that representative democracy is complemented by direct democratic elements with decision power. In the longer term, it may decide to strive for the introduction of a general direct democracy.

Of course, it would also be conceivable to extend the voting basis to the entire population. This would come very close to the introduction of direct democracy. The systems would only have to be accessible for the entire population accordingly. However, this approach has decisive disadvantages:

- How does the party ensure whether there is a real person behind the respective user (instead of a bot)?
- How does the party ensure that a user does not obtain several votes by fraud?
- How does the party determine whether the user is entitled to vote in the respective election?

By restricting voting rights to members of the proxy party, a positive self-selection of politically interested people is achieved. They are far more interested in politics itself and in active participation than the average population. They inform themselves more intensively about voting issues and are therefore able to make better decisions.

A different solution for creating the Party Program

The German Initiative "Basisdemokratie Jetzt!" (Grassroot Democracy Now!) offers a different approach. It aims to unite all smaller German democratic political parties under an 'umbrella party' making it more achievable to reach the 5% election outcome which is set as a hurdle for seats in parliaments. Each party can decide from election to election on the local/regional/state/country level if it wants to run under the flag of the umbrella party or under its own flag. In case of a successful election, the parliamentary seats and the state subsidies are allocated to the participating parties.

To achieve the widest basis of agreement for a party program for this umbrella party, the approach 'simply' combines the existing party programs. When comparing the different parties' programs, the picture roughly looks like the following:

- About 60% of the parties' programs are based on the same principles (they merge together)
- About 30% of the parties' programs complement the other parties' programs, e.g. one party that has the topic of a Universal Basic Income and the party that focuses on animal rights (both are added to the program)
- About 10% of the parties' programs are contradictory (these topics will be discussed and in case of no agreement by the parties decided upon by the members of all of the participating parties)

In reality, the wording for the 60% will still have to be discussed, the added 30% will also have to make sense for the other parties, and the 10% might mean that a party will choose not to join.

According to the founder Günther Ziethoff, the major advantage of this organic approach is that "the new program is a natural merge of the existing programs and easier to agree on for the members of the participating political parties."

It is very positive that the different approaches to problem-solving as a basis for discussion lead to a cross-party political opinion-forming process.

The difficulty with this approach lies in the distribution of successes, since it will be very difficult to determine the share of success each small party had in the overall success of the umbrella party. However, the founder Günther Ziethoff has also developed a model for this that includes voter stars, top candidates of each party and a proportional distribution.

A potential disadvantage is that the parties might not be incentivized to fully discuss the urgently required structural changes for politics and its laws and rules as precondition for a better representation and fairer rules. Even if one party brings this deep analysis and solutions to the merged program with its party program, it seems to be seen if the other parties' members will intensively discuss these topics and stand behind them.

Another possible disadvantage is that small parties that do not accept the so-called 'code of ethics' or the common 'fundamental values' are perceived as 'undemocratic' and are therefore not allowed to participate. However, this can also be an advantage due to the resulting internal lower friction within the umbrella party.

Why isn't it enough to vote for individual proxy members?
The alternative to the Proxy Party would be individual candidates who see themselves as directly elected Proxy Representatives. They would be normally elected as direct candidates and would vote exactly as their voters determine.

In the US, there are already candidates who have promised to behave in elections as determined by their voters through a platform such as united.vote[37] or other digital platforms.[38] One of them is David Ernst.[39] The book *Architecture of a Technodemocracy* outlines a framework for a democracy based on individual candidates.

At first glance, these directly elected individual proxy candidates are a good idea. They correspond to the ideal of direct democracy. But this direct election has some disadvantages that majorly result from the current state of the political system:

1. In many countries, the approach of direct candidates would only aim at winning half of the parliamentary seats. The other half is determined by the overall percentage the party achieves in the election.

2. The single candidate system will take into account only the majority of a single constituency. This may result in the will of the voters not being expressed. Example: three constituencies with 100% and 49% and 48% approval. Result: one vote for and two votes against, although almost two out of three voters agree with the proposal.

3. Individual candidates will be less successful in activating many voters and integrating them into everyday political life.

4. The individual candidate will not be able to create many good quality templates to discuss them with his voters. He simply lacks the time and resources. If this work can be distributed among several people, more can be done.

5. One candidate alone has a far lower chance of attracting experts to provide better input and lead discussions.

6. An individual candidate will be dependent on external systems. As an individual, he is not in a position to advance the development of platforms that he needs for efficient exchange with his voters.

7. An individual candidate will have less changes to invest in systems that ensure that only registered voters (e.g. citizen of the city) vote and that they only cast one vote.

8. Individual candidates can be more easily ignored than a party that has passed the 5% hurdle. They can spread the idea of direct democracy and transparency less successfully than an entire party that focuses on these issues.

Does the idea of the Proxy Party work for countries with a two-party-system like the US and UK?

According to a 2018 poll, 57% of Americans judged the Republican and Democratic parties to do such a poor job that a third major party is needed.[40] So there seems to be a justification for a third party to exist.

But at first glance, it doesn't look pretty for a third party. Voting for third party candidates often means that you 'waste your vote'. Your candidate stands no chance against the candidates of the larger parties. In the US presidential election, this means not giving the 'party you dislike less' your vote, which might lead to your 'worst choice' being elected. As already described, this leads to a 'tactical vote' and heavily favors the two large parties and their candidates.

But what if the 42% of American voters registered as independent[41] would see a real chance for a new start? A fresh start with a new party really representing them and not the 0.05% spending more than $10,000 in political campaigns.

If you widen your view you can see the full picture that politicians don't like to mention:

- The voter turnout in the UK general election was only 68.8%. The leading conservative party only received 5.7% more than the non-voters group.[42]
- The voter turnout in the 2017 US presidential election was only 58%.[43] The largest group was the group of non-voters!

But why does this large group choose not to vote? Three primary reasons:

1.   They don't care enough about politics.

2.   They don't think that their vote can lead to any real change.

3.   They don't want to lend the corrupt system credibility by giving their vote.

But what if those non-voters:

> …would recognize that the new type of party is their only chance for a real democracy?
>
> …would see a real chance not to 'waste' their votes because ranked-choice got introduced so that they can safely vote for their real preference and not strategically?
>
> …would know that the election of the new party puts power in their hands?
>
> …vote two thirds in favor of the new party?
>
> …would half vote for the new party, along with some other voters who are tired of the established parties?

What if a new US party would choose to run on what most Americans actually want, like the more than 40 topics listed in the ARC article from Renae Marshall?[44]

"One of the many people who live in a State or a District where your vote has never made a difference? Join the Liquid Democracy Party and as long as we have at least one representative from somewhere — you have regained some portion of your sovereignty."[45]

What about the cooperation between Proxy Parties of different nations?

Because it works fact-based and outcome focused, the Proxy Party is always interested in working with partners who can reliably support it in collecting and checking facts. It will be happy to work with other Proxy Parties on a national and international level, because they have committed themselves to similar ground rules.

The cooperation with other proxy parties is useful in many areas, among others an exchange of information …

> … about secured facts and fact checks for topics for the preparation of discussions and decisions (incl. successively building a solid knowledge base)
>
> … on the experience of parties from other countries in implementing policies, and their actual costs and effects.
>
> … on the experiences with different inner-party processes etc.

This model would offer a far more cooperative and efficient alternative to the current political system. This will enable better cooperation between nations in the medium term, which is urgently needed in order to successfully tackle common problems.

Is the Proxy Party the best option for democracy?
In my opinion, the proxy party is just the best option that can be implemented as the next step in the current situation. The Proxy Party is only an intermediate stage in the development of democracy.

How the next step will look like, will mainly depend on the popularity of the Proxy Party or similar basic democratic models and their experiences. As an inspiration, I would like to refer to the bottom-up approach of Klaas Mensaert's 'inclusive party'. This would completely dissolve the current party oligopoly, provide us with an anti-fragile democratic system, greatly reduce the current polarization and allow for better cooperation. In his book *The Flaws that Kill Our Democracy*, he argues well why the current approach of 'exclusive parties' leads to polarization, a large accumulation of power, little innovation and instability of the entire political system. The two main components of his approach are:

- Party representatives: Legislation proposed by hundreds of inclusive parties, more akin to our current communities of interest, each with only one representative.
- People's representatives: Decisions on proposed laws by impartial representatives of the people directly appointed by the people, protected from influence like judges

ENDING POLITICAL APATHY

I hope I succeeded in outlining a cohesive and realistic way to create a new breed of political party as a democratic parliamentarian champion: a party that is grassroot democratic yet effective and efficient. Following the advice of Buckminster Fuller, it creates a new and far better alternative to represent us in parliament and replace the old political parties.

Of cause, the sketch provided in this short book can be only a start. Rules and processes will have to be refined and tested and optimized. The new culture and principles will have to be cultivated and implemented on a broad scale.

Culture, principles, rules, and processes combined will ensure that the Proxy Party can't warp into the stuff the normal political party is made from. It will stay true to democracy, transparency, and representation.

I invite you to imagine a political party...

> ... that asks you for your input and actually listens to it.
> ... that will focus on the priorities of its members.
> ... that is concentrated to find underlying checked facts before discussing solutions.
> ... that is interested in letting us know the whole story about the problems instead of giving us its own one-sided view of things.
> ... that only supports the individual political decision-making process of its members instead of prescribing it.
> ... that leaves the important decision to its members (if they want)
> ... that is truly transparent and can prove it walks the talk.

... that is focused to represent the will of its member base as exactly as possible.

We can make this true. We can upgrade democracy.

We just have to put trust in ourselves and our fellow citizens (and design the system well) to be successful and change the world for the better, instead of watching the creeping dismantling of democracy.

> "A great democracy has got to be progressive
> or it will soon too cease to be great or a democracy."
> -Theodore Roosevelt

Thanks for reading my book! I would be very pleased if you would give me honest feedback on my book, my thoughts, and the idea of the Proxy Party. What was the favorite thing you took away from the book?

Your review will also help other readers find my book and the ideas.

If you like, you can also visit me on my website upgradingdemocracy.com to learn more about the idea.

Thank you!

-Peter

P.S.: A successful implementation also includes supporting IT systems. If you are interested, take a look at the appendix in which I have defined the requirements for such a system. I am currently thinking about the implementation of a DLT-based system. If you want to participate, you are welcome to send me an email to contact@upgradingdemocracy.com.

APPENDIX

MINI PUBLICS ADDING TO DEMOCRACY

Democracy tends to work poorly when individuals solely reach a judgement on their own. If individuals do not feel the need to articulate their ideas and to test, and if necessary, correct them by exchanging them with others, there is no deliberation, but just a vote. But, only the view out of one's own filter bubble and a discourse can lead to an increase in knowledge about the respective topic, its mechanisms, and an understanding of the positions of others.

But who has the time to inform himself intensively about all political topics and to form a well-founded opinion on them? This is the only convincing argument a representation by a smaller group of delegates who represent the electorate as a whole and make decisions for it. This group can focus fully on the issues and will therefore be able to achieve better thought-out results.

The decisive factor for success is the calm, fact-based exchange between the participants. New opinions can be formed in an open and safe climate. In order to achieve this working atmosphere, it is important to agree in advance on a number of basic principles such as transparency, fairness, equality of votes, efficiency, respect and collegiality.[46]

Most of us only know parliamentary democracy with its parties and their professional politicians as their representatives. Historically however, there are other models that have been very successful. Particularly, the allocation of a large proportion of public offices by lot. This type of democratic representation was e.g. practiced in Athens and during the Renaissance in the city-states of Venice and Florence.

In the last two decades, the use of these models has led to many positive experiences worldwide. So-called 'mini-publics,' have been used to discuss complex problems and propose solutions. The participants of these groups, who are to represent the public, are drawn by lot according to their characteristics (age, gender, educational level, etc.). They form a smaller representative picture of the population. If one citizen refuses to participate in the group, the next citizen with similar characteristics will be drawn.

In the processes the group is supported by professional facilitators. The information required for assessment is obtained by citizens through hearing and consultation of experts and representatives of all relevant stakeholders. These are not present during the evaluation work. The results of the group's consultations are summarized in a citizens' report. This is made available to the political decision-making bodies as a consultation document.

The mini publics are primarily intended to provide a sheltered space. A limited number of citizens receive balanced information. Deliberative discussions with fellow citizens from different social groups are encouraged. This is mainly achieved by:

a)   the selection of participants that represents a representative cross-section of the population and enabling them to exchange views on the subject with persons from entirely different socio-economic backgrounds.

b)   a careful selection of witnesses which is made so that the participants are informed in a balanced way about the relevant issues.

c)   the facilitators ensuring that the very different participants meet with mutual respect and ensure that citizens hear the contributions of all participants during the deliberations.[47]

This format has already been used in many situations to make representative decisions in complex situations. Well-known examples with different varieties of 'mini-publics' are the referendum in Ireland in 2018 (including abortion law), the citizens' assembly of the Canadian province of British Columbia, which took place in 2004 to reform the electoral law, the "Citizens' Initiative Review Process" of the US state of Oregon and the participatory budgeting of Porto Alegre in Brazil. Further examples and the working methods of these planning cells and citizens' assemblies are presented on americaspeaks.org and in my book *Upgrading Democracy*.

SAVE AND USABLE TECH

The chapter is primarily intended for readers who are interested in IT systems and know that they are essential for the successful implementation of the idea. In the following, based on the ideas in this book, I will try to sketch the components of a system that will be crucial for success. These are only a first draft and still need many improvements.

Proxy Party systems must cover the following functions, which can be divided into seven main areas:

1. **Authentication** of members and other users, including assignment of rights for constituencies and topics.

2. **Administration** of members and their rights and roles in the system.

3. **Activation** of as many members as possible. Motivate them to participate in the process. Activation of external experts.

4. **Collaboration and Collective Sense Making** - Joint collection and prioritization of issues, facts and review of these, creation of a wiki of already validated knowledge. Process of effective and efficient consultation with the aim of gaining knowledge for the participants and creating a common basis incl. graphic representation for better visualization of topics. Joint creation of decision templates.

5. **Voting** with various forms of delegation to individuals or groups in the style of a liquid democracy with a 24-hour advance warning for delegated votes.

A system to give members a preset number of votes each month, which they can use for thematic votes. Options for counting votes: Stable votes or votes shrinking in value over time, quadratic voting.

6. **Distribution of Members' votes** to elected representatives for their voting in parliament, achieving a 1:1 representation including minimization of coercion and an even distribution of this democratic burden on Members[48]

7. **Usability** - The system must be easy to use, so that even new members can quickly find their way around and make the best use of the system.

The system must also be verifiable on a source code basis and therefore open source.

1. Authentication

Authentication is a critical component of the system. The party must ensure that each member is a natural person and only has one vote. It will also have to check that the member is a citizen of the voting district or state and can be given according to voting rights.

In German-speaking countries there is a simple solution, the 'Post-Ident procedure' or newer online alternatives. Combined with a direct debit authorization from an account, it is doubly secured that it is the person indicated.

There is no simple solution for countries with no central identity card requirement or if the 'Post-Ident procedure' should not be chosen. A central solution is too vulnerable as it can be hacked. The best solution would be a decentralized solution combined with an official sign-off from a public authority for the information that can be found on an Identity Card and the eligibility to vote in a certain district, etc.

This is a very complex problem with no 100% solution in sight.

The most promising solution I came across up so far is described in a white paper[48] from Nicole Immorlica, Matthew O. Jackson, and Glen Weyl, which takes 'Intersectional Identities' as a basis for the required proof. Their work refers back to the social reality of pre-formal identity. Identity then was a network of interpersonal direct or indirect knowledge about other persons. From the point of view of the authors, the crucial aspects of identity are redundancy, sociality and intersectionality:

> Redundancy: a person is uniquely defined by a set of features and past interactions. Even a subset of this unique set is sufficient to identify her. This implies that an individuum only has to give away a small part of her

identity to authenticate herself. Identity theft is much harder to pull off than in the current centralized systems.

Sociality: most of the data that uniquely defines a person is by its nature shared with others and known by others. This starts with the date of birth known by your parents and the doctor and nurses but is also valid for working with co-workers, in-person discussions, etc. This implies that normally "it is usually sufficient for that individual to use preexisting social sharing of data, thereby largely avoiding compromises of privacy or security."[49]

Intersectionality: the individual can in large parts be seen "as intersection of the social groups with whom the constituents of her identity are shared."[50] This enables the individual to rely on a range of different social connections to avoid making any individual or group a central chokepoint.

This approach can be combined with physical meetings to sign other individuals' cryptographic keys that serve as a proxy for identity. "Keys with many trusted signatures are themselves trusted and can be used as proof of identity."[51] The more facts a key signed off that later are deemed to be useful and truthful, the more additional trustworthiness is accumulated by this key.

Local meetings of party members of the Proxy Party can be used to link a name, citizenship and a location to a cryptographic key. A hash function that transforms the original data into an alphanumeric code that changes very noticeably with the smallest changes to the original would enable the detection of double entries as members of the Proxy Party. The process of signing of person data as seen on an official document can be split up in several steps. This avoids that a 'stranger' sees the complete data on your identity card.

2. Administration of members

- Member administration
  - Identity system (see above)
  - Membership fee administration (incl. reduced fees, waiver of fees, self-chosen fees)
  - ...
- Role and rights system
- Expert Status System, Expert Profiles and Talent Pool: System for obtaining expert status, checking and granting expert status for specific topics

- Organization of conferences and meetings
- Group Calendar
- File repository
- Further suggestions: see Piratenwiki

3. Activation of Members

Activation of as many party members as possible for active and positive participation in the party's processes as well as external subject experts.

- Tagging and alert system for matching topics and member interests, knowledge and commitment, so that each user is addressed to the topics relevant to him or her and is motivated to become more intensively involved in them.
- Notification of successes, updates etc.
- Invitation to local meetings
- Invitation to votes and elections
- Surveys
- (Personalized) Newsletter

4. Collaboration and collective sense making

The technical systems must enable an efficient cooperation, especially the collection and prioritization of topics and the deliberation processes.

- Reputation system to recognize, reward and incentivize behavior that benefits the party: win new members, take part in deliberation, facilitate, add facts, fact check, cocreate the topic interdependency chart, contribute to party Wiki, create slogans and memes, create graphics, write software, etc.
- Efficient topic identification and deliberation

  - Voting on topics and their inclusion: dimensions: 'Importance'/ 'Importance' and 'Urgency'. Gradual inclusion and involvement of larger groups of members, e.g. 1%, 5%, 25% of the members, whereby there must be at least one intermediate stage before the topic is communicated to all members. Listing according to the number of votes achieved. (see "Voting System").

  - Inclusion of new topics including the creation of structured topic proposals and tagging (see above).

  - Structured collection of verified facts and influencing factors as well as quality assurance.

- Mechanisms to enable effective and efficient counselling with the aim of gaining knowledge for the participants and to create a common basis, including graphic presentation for faster access to complex topics (see example systems below) and the creation of a Wiki as common knowledge base.
- Text length limit for posts per user per discussion.
- System for evaluating user actions for their valuable contributions (new fact, new connection, better understanding, etc.), linking this 'knowledge growth feedback' to the possibility of entering additional texts and the possibility of achieving expert status.
- System that allows users to tag (see Tagging System) posts and group posts into a connecting topic. Rewarding work with permission to enter more text on a topic.
- Mechanisms for exclusion of users in case of violation. Exclusion for a defined period of time depending on the severity of the violation.

- Voting Material Preparation
    - Preparation of the topic template (intro, facts, mechanisms, pros, cons, recommendations)
    - Deliberation on the basis of the topic template
    - Release of the discussion template as decision basis according to the threshold value (e.g. expert opinions account for 50% of the weighting, alternatively only separate display of expert opinions)
    - Sortition of randomly selected members by certain criteria (gender, age, education, etc.) to create a 'mini public'
    - Evaluation of the participants (split by: expert, normal participant), how satisfied they are with preparation of the topic (all important facets correctly presented, fair well-balanced presentation of the topic)
- Coordination of active party members
    - Expert profiles: system to receive expert credentials for certain topic areas, check them and grant expert status for certain topics
    - Limitation of the text length for contributions per user
    - System for evaluating user actions for their valuable contributions (new fact, new connection, better understanding, etc.), linking this 'knowledge growth feedback' to the possibility of further text input

Voting system

- Voting system

  - Voting system with the following options: 'normal voting' with one vote per person per vote/ 'system with voting points' distributed each week or month of membership for thematic votes (including a freely selectable devaluation factor for these accumulated votes)

  - Voting options for candidates and topics: Classical selection of one or more voting options/ Voting for each voting option from -1 to +1 in steps of 0.1 or 0.25/ Voting for each voting option: absolute against/ against/ neutral/ supportive/ fully supportive.

- Delegation system and elections.

  - An opportunity to rank up to ten candidates or proposed solutions in an election. System to sort out the candidate/ solution with the lowest vote score from the list and allocate the votes this option received as first choice to the second-choice option of these voters etc. (ranked-choice voting)

  - Delegation of votes for subject areas or individual votes or candidates to persons or groups

  - A system to connect votes to group decisions when delegated to a group (majority vote or 1:1 passing of votes)

  - Alert to the voter who delegated his vote 24 hours before the vote: how would his delegated vote currently vote (the uncertainty about the potential further delegation of the vote does not violate voting secrecy)

  - User can overwrite his vote at any time (until the last minute)

  - Based on Blockchain or another secure Decentralized Ledger Technology

- Analysis of the election

  - Verification that the integrity of the vote has been maintained

  - Counting according to a pre-defined procedure

  - Determination of the election result

  - Verification, if the integrity of the vote-counting was maintained according to the specified procedure

Vote allocation

- Allocation of voting shares to elected representatives according to their own preferences and the distribution of the member votes
- Minimization of the difference from the personal choices of the representatives and the vote they are ordered to take on behalf of the party

Usability

A good system must provide a very good user experience. For the system of the Proxy Party, this means that even a new member should be able to easily orient himself, understand his options, understand the culture and the rules, can easily drill down topics and related material, take part in the discussion and give feedback, can connect with other members and understand his options to vote and those for delegation. At least it shouldn't take very long to learn to interact with the system.

All actions should be also usable with a mobile interface. This will pose challenges, especially with complex topics and their graphical representation.

Some systems to keep an eye on

Some interesting systems, which have already implemented part of the requirements outlined above:

Graphical Representation: https://www.kialo.com/, inilab.ch, https://consider.it/, https://pol.is/home, https://democracy.foundation/deliberation-in-epitome/

Fact-Checking: http://crowdfact.io/

Organizations/ Communities and Voting:
https://liqd.net/en/software, https://www.agora.vote, https://nativeproject.one/, https://dcentproject.eu/, http://democracyos.org/, https://democracy.foundation/cycles/, https://www.airesis.eu/eparticipation, https://citizenos.com/, https://decidim.org/features/, https://yrpri.org/, https://crowdpol.com/, https://consulproject.org/en/, https://adhocracy.plus/

Blockchain Protocols/ Solutions: Sovereign by https://democracy.earth, https://aragon.org, https://commonsstack.org[52], https://blog.colony.io

Decentralized Ledger Protocols (DLTs): https://holochain.org

A list with over 50 open source solutions <u>be found on democracy.foundation.</u>

#####

I am currently in the process of thinking more deeply about the implementation of the system just described and creating mock-ups for it. These should then be implemented on the basis of decentralized ledger technologies (DLT).

AUTHOR BIOGRAPHY

Peter Monien is a 'political refugee' from Germany who lives in Switzerland. He has become increasingly disenchanted with what politicians are deciding in the name of the people and are doing with public funds, mostly unknown to the electorates they pretend to represent. After the 2007 financial crisis (and the subsequent lack of accountability at every economic and political level), he has lost faith in mainstream politics.

Peter's attempts to understand what led to these catastrophic outcomes, which are evidently not in the best interests of the average citizen, drove him to become a systems thinker in order to better understand the complex interrelated and interdependent parts of our political systems, with a view to effecting urgent change.

In August 2018, Peter decided to step forward and develop a new, truly democratic counterproposal to the current entrenched political system.

This journey led him over the political precipice and into the abyss of current political systems, arriving at an analysis of their weaknesses in order to propose a range of possible solutions that play to the strengths of true democracy.

The results of his research and proposal for a new kind of grassroots democratic political party, the 'Proxy Party,' can be found in his book *Upgrading Democracy* and this book *Achieving True Democracy*.

Peter's broad background in banking, economics, business administration, including market development and sales, gives him a unique insight into business and communications systems. As systems thinker and co-founder and former board member of the largest German freelancer cooperative, Peter is uniquely equipped to formulate and deploy actionable ideas that positively impact large-scale organizations, institutions and processes. Since 2014, he has been looking into how decentralized systems can be applied to achieve these goals for a fairer and more egalitarian society.

WEBSITE AND SOCIAL MEDIA COORDINATES

Website https://upgradingdemocracy.com/

Twitter:
https://twitter.com/peter_monien and https://twitter.com/waytodemocracy

Pinterest https://www.pinterest.de/UpgradingDemocracy/boards/

YouTube https://www.youtube.com/channel/UCo4tzHoiaGRQce-Apgl2bGA

Medium https://medium.com/@pmonien[1]

SOURCES

[1] https://arcdigital.media/what-if-a-presidential-candidate-ran-on-what-most-americans-actually-wanted-bd570321b428

[2] https://press.princeton.edu/books/paperback/9780691162423/affluence-and-influence

[3] http://www.armuts-und-reichtumsbericht.de/SharedDocs/Downloads/Service/Studien/endbericht-systematisch-verzerrte-entscheidungen.pdf The original uncensored report mentioned a "crisis of reputation". See comparison of the versions by Lobby Control: https://www.lobbycontrol.de/wp-content/uploads/LobbyControl-Vorher-Nachher-Vergleich-Armutsbericht.pdf

[4] Global Satisfaction with Democracy Report 2020, https://www.cam.ac.uk/system/files/report2020_003.pdf, p.9.

[5] Tony Bracks, Solving for Democracy, p. 241

[6] Upgrading Democracy: Claiming a Say to Achieve True Democracy, Peter Monien, p. 116

[7] The Three Languages of Politics: Talking Across the Political Divides, Arnold Kling

[8] Upgrading Democracy: Claiming a Say to Achieve True Democracy, Peter Monien, p. 118

[9] Nordic Ideology, Hanzi Freinacht, p. 190-191

[10] Nordic Ideology, Hanzi Freinacht, p. 47

[11] Liquid Reign, Tim Reutemann and Karl-Heinz Häsliprinz, p. 118

[12] Bruce Bueno de Mescita, The Dictator's Handbook, p. 281

[13] Wait But Why, A Sick Giant, graphic: https://www.pinterest.de/pin/560135272407814357/

[14] Nordic Ideology, Hanzi Freinacht, p. 53

[15] http://xk.io/2017/05/27/ibdd-and-poppers-criterion/

[16] https://wbj.pl/hungary-first-arrests-for-spreading-fake-news/post/127074

[17] https://ipi.media/european-media-freedom-suffers-covid-19-response/

[18] https://ipi.media/european-media-freedom-suffers-covid-19-response/

[19] Translated from German: Jens Wernicke, Lügen die Medien? Propaganda, Rudeljournalismus und der Kampf um die öffentliche Meinung, p. 139, Rainer Mausfeld

[20] Translated from German: Jens Wernicke, p. 32, David Goeßmann

[21] https://www.bariweiss.com/resignation-letter

[22] Translated from German: Rainer Mausfeld, Warum schweigen die Lämmer?: Wie Elitendemokratie und Neoliberalismus unsere Gesellschaft und unsere Lebensgrundlagen bedrohen, Position 519

[23] https://youtu.be/ii5MlQgGXyk, Empire Files Episode 79 - An Ocean of Lies on Venezuela: Abby Martin & UN Rapporteur Expose Coup

[24] Translated from German: Jens Wernicke, p. 70, Ulrich Tilgner

[25] Translated from German: Jens Wernicke, p. 80, Stephan Hebel

[26] Censored, Paul Coleman, Pos. 1773

[27] Translated from German: https://youtu.be/W2WkPolNDtI?t=1283, Wissensmanufaktur, Prof. Norbert Bolz: Der Journalist als Oberlehrer

[28] Translated from German: https://youtu.be/W2WkPolNDtI?t=2081, see above Wissensmanufaktur

[29] Translated from German: https://youtu.be/W2WkPolNDtI?t=2280, see above Wissensmanufaktur

[30] Translated from German: https://youtu.be/W2WkPolNDtI?t=2760, see above Wissensmanufaktur

[31] Translated from German: https://youtu.be/W2WkPolNDtI?t=2990, see above Wissensmanufaktur

[32] http://humanetech.com/wp-content/uploads/2019/07/CHT-Undivided-Attention-Podcast-Ep.4-Down-the-Rabbit-Hole.pdf, p. 6

[33] https://waitbutwhy.com/2019/12/political-disney-world.html

[34] https://samharris.org/podcasts/152-trouble-facebook/

[35] https://www.forbes.com/sites/robtoews/2020/05/25/deepfakes-are-going-to-wreak-havoc-on-society-we-are-not-prepared/ and https://www.digitaltrends.com/features/audio-deepfakes-recording-industry/

[36] https://medium.com/thewashingtonpost/top-ai-researchers-race-to-detect-deepfake-videos-we-are-outgunned-ce4c057b0625 and
https://twimlai.com/twiml-talk-260-fighting-fake-news-and-deep-fakes-with-machine-learning-w-delip-rao/ starting from min. 30:29

[37] https://liquid.us

[38] https://medium.com/@dallasjcole/kavanaugh-circus-is-latest-example-of-how-winner-take-all-decisions-warp-our-democracy-cb882a363c20

[39] https://techcrunch.com/2018/02/24/liquid-democracy-uses-blockchain

[40] https://news.gallup.com/poll/244094/majority-say-third-party-needed.aspx

[41] Unbreaking America: A NEW Short Film about Solving the Corruption Crisis, https://youtu.be/TfQij4aQq1k

[42] https://en.wikipedia.org/wiki/2017_United_Kingdom_general_election

[43] https://guides.libraries.psu.edu/post-election-2016/voter-turnout

[44] https://arcdigital.media/what-if-a-presidential-candidate-ran-on-what-most-americans-actually-wanted-bd570321b428

[45] https://medium.com/emergent-culture/we-can-restore-democracy-by-disrupting-politics-here-is-how-c9d514a8c194

[46] Translated from German: mdmagazin, Ausgabe 1.2019, Seite 11

[47] Graham Smith, Democratic Innovations: Designing Institutions for Citizen Participation (Theories of Institutional Design), p. 174

[48] https://papers.ssrn.com/sol3/papers.cfm?abstract_id=3375436

[49] Nicole Immorlica, Matthew O. Jackson, Glen Weyl, Verifying Identity as a Social Intersection, p. 2

[50] Nicole Immorlica, p. 2

[51] Nicole Immorlica, p. 6

[52] https://medium.com/giveth/introducing-the-commons-stack-scalable-infrastructure-for-community-collaboration-6886eb97413e